Christopher RADKO'S

ORNAMENTS

Christopher RADKO'S

ORNAMENTS

Text by Olivia Bell Buehl

Clarkson Potter/Publishers

NEW YORK

- - - - - - - - - - - - - - - - - -

- - - - - - - - - - - - - - - - - -

✳

Published by Clarkson Potter/Publishers, 201 East 50th Street, New York, New York 10022. Member of the Crown Publishing Group.

- - - - - - - - - - - - - - - - - -

Random House, Inc. New York, Toronto, London, Sydney, Auckland
www.randomhouse.com

✳

CLARKSON POTTER, POTTER,
and colophon are registered trademarks of Random House, Inc.

- - - - - - - - - - - - - - - - - -

Printed in the United States of America

DESIGN BY JILL ARMUS

✳

Library of Congress Cataloging-in-Publication Data
Radko, Christopher.
Christopher Radko's ornaments / text by Olivia Bell Buehl.—1st ed.
1. Radko, Christopher—Themes, motifs.   2. Glass Christmas decorations—United States—Themes, motifs.   I. Radko, Christopher.   II. Title.
III. Title: Ornaments.
NK5198.R33A4   1999
748.8—dc21   99-14443

- - - - - - - - - - - - - - - - - -

ISBN 0-609-60476-7

- - - - - - - - - - - - - - - - - -

10 9 8 7 6 5 4 3 2 1

- - - - - - - - - - - - - - - - - -

First Edition

ACKNOWLEDGMENTS

T HIS BOOK would not have been possible without the help of many talented people. First, I'd like to extend my appreciation to both my office and showroom staff who gladly pitched in on top of their already heavy regular duties: Kyle Hall, Janet Bucknor, Sue Ameijide, Rose-anne Macari, Ron Hendon, Bill Rhodes, Sharon Miller, and Pamela Kantor. Their individual talents united to create a superb group effort. Timothy Scalet and Cole Nagy, of my visual merchandising team, worked their magic for photographs by Kelly Budgen of Christmas trees and other decorations.

Special kudos to John O'Donnell for his superb photographs of the ornaments. Reflective glass objects are notoriously difficult to record, but John's skill, ingenuity, and plain good nature overcame any technical challenges to produce images that capture the essence of each work.

Many thanks to my editor, Margot Schupf, who had the vision to imagine this book and the fortitude to guide its journey to the printed page, and to the rest of the team at Clarkson Potter—Lauren Shakely, Mark McCauslin, Marysarah Quinn, Maggie Hinders, Jane Searle, Jean Lynch, and Tom Zuk. Special thanks to Jill Armus for her beautiful design.

Steve Robba graciously lent his expertise on the secondary market in Christopher Radko ornaments.

My collaborator Olivia Bell Buehl went to the heart of the matter, researching the history of Christmas and glass ornaments as well as probing into the inspiration and process involved in producing my creations. Her text is a wonderful complement to the ornaments themselves.

Finally, my deep gratitude to the many collectors who have made my ornaments an integral part of their family celebrations of Christmas—and of other holidays, too. Their loyalty and encouragement inspire me each day as I seek new ways to share the joy and heart of Christmas.

CONTENTS

PREFACE

OR MANY PEOPLE, Christmas is exclusively the observance of religious customs celebrating the birth of Christ. But to me, Christmas transcends the rituals and observances that happen on just one single day in December. It is also about the here and now. It is about reconnecting with your friends and family, about spending time with and opening yourself to people, and extending your heart to the whole family of mankind. The emphasis is not solely on the Nativity as an event, but on what the season means to people and what it means to internalize and live the message of light and hope and love.

I'd like to help those qualities be part of our day-to-day lives. The season's message is heart based, not religious. You can be of any religion or no religion and still have heart. My ornaments convey this message, because they too are heart based. They come from the core of my being, and that's why people respond to them so strongly.

Ornaments are a link to past holidays that evoke warm memories of our loved ones and friends. Since Christmas is about sharing memories and traditions, the Christmas tree is the centerpiece of those emotions. A tree is more than a thing of wonder, although wondrous it is; it is also a diary of your family's history. Each ornament tells a different story.

My goal is to lift people's spirits, to make ornaments that bring joy, light, and mirth into their lives year-round. Ornaments can serve as a trigger to recall with whom you shared a certain holiday, or who gave you that wonderful gift.

You are reminded of that dear person every year when you hang that sparkling gift on the tree once again. In a way, ornaments are physical manifestations of priceless moments with our loved ones.

If you believe in magic, as I do, you believe that the ornaments carry good wishes. I send my creations out into the universe with a mission to touch people's hearts, to carry the message of love and joy to those who receive them. Sometimes late at night, when everyone else has gone home and I'm the last one in the warehouse, I stand in front of the latest shipment from Europe, and I say to my ornaments, "Hey, guys, I've brought you into the world. Now go out and share your magic with others." I've loved them and nurtured them, but I know that now it is time for them to go forth in all different directions. They will hang on trees in homes and other places that I may never get to visit,

but through my ornaments, my heart will be there.

The European artisans with whom I work have this craft in their blood, in their bones. They're sharing creations that they are honored to make and proud to have in their homes—they celebrate Christmas with the self-same ornaments they make for me. The spirit of the craftsman is in each ornament, as it is born with love and literally with the breath of a human being. Through the ornaments' sparkle, their inner glow, I am able to share the heart of Christmas.

It is wonderful to see the great-grandchildren of the original glassblowers following once again their family heritage. It might have skipped a generation or two because of the wars and the hardships under Communism, but to regain, to reconnect with, a turn-of-the-century craft that your grandparents were involved with is very meaningful. I have a warm sense of satisfaction that I was able to sponsor that reconnection, that revival, that lost link for many of these people. I love bringing new life to old things. And I think that is what I have done with my Christmas ornaments: I've given an all but extinct tradition of mouth-blown glass creations a new lease on life, and ensured that it will endure into the next millennium.

These decorations are more than ornamental—not just works of art, they are works of heart!

—CHRISTOPHER RADKO

Introduction

A BRIEF
HISTORY OF
GLASS
ORNAMENTS

RHINELAND MAGIC

REALLY THREE ORNAMENTS IN ONE, A PAIR OF "ROSY LOVEBIRDS" PERCH ON A ROSE WITH A REFLECTOR IN ITS CENTER, *BELOW*. SIMILAR ROSES (WITHOUT REFLECTORS) ONCE HELD CHRISTMAS CANDLES. BIRDS ARE JOINED TO THE FLOWER WITH SPRINGS SO THEY CAN BOB AND FLUTTER REALISTICALLY. THE CLIP-ON ORNAMENT TYPIFIES THE HIGH QUALITY OF TRADITIONAL GERMAN ORNAMENT MOLDS.

IKE THE whimsical figure we know today as Santa Claus and the charming custom of decorating an evergreen tree, glass ornaments originated in Germany in the early part of the nineteenth century as an outgrowth of the toy industry. The first glass ornaments were free-blown globes, ovals, teardrops, balls, and other relatively simple shapes.

Egyptians had invented the art of glassblowing almost five thousand years before, and Roman soldiers spread the skill as they conquered northern lands. Since 1597 Lauscha, a town in Germany's Thuringian mountains, has been a center for glassmaking. By the early eighteenth century, Lauscha was supplying glass beads for jewelers and milliners all over Europe. In 1857, rival glassblowers in Bohemia, now the Czech Republic, developed a silver nitrate solution that coated the insides of their beads, much like the coated back of a mirror, giving them a reflective brilliance and luster. Spurred by this competition, the Lauschans developed similar technology. Meanwhile, by the middle of the nineteenth century—an 1848 purchase order confirms that date—it was discovered that glass could be blown into a mold to create figures.

THE CAT'S MEOW

"KITTY CLAUS," *TOP LEFT*, IS
BLOWN FROM AN OLD GERMAN
MOLD. CHARMING DETAILS
INCLUDE THE EARS POKING OUT
THE FRONT OF ITS STOCKING
CAP, THE NECK RIBBON, AND THE
SKILLFULLY APPLIED WHISKERS
AND EYELASHES.

✳

VINTAGE DESIGNS

"PINING SANTA," *TOP RIGHT*,
BASED ON AN OLD GERMAN
MOLD, COMES IN FOUR JEWEL-
TONE COLORS. ANOTHER CLASSIC
GERMAN ORNAMENT, DATING TO
THE EARLY 1900S, "KAISER PIPE,"
LEFT, SEAMLESSLY JOINS THE
MOLDED PORTRAIT OF KAISER
WILHELM ON THE BOWL WITH
THE FREEFORM GLASS STEM.
"BIRDHOUSE," *BOTTOM LEFT*, AN
EARLY LAUSCHAN MOLD DEPICT-
ING A CARDINAL AND BLUEBIRD
TAKING REFUGE UNDER A
THATCH-ROOFED STRUCTURE,
SYMBOLIZES THE SANCTITY
OF A HAPPY HOME.

TWO PLUS
TWO

THE TEARDROP-SHAPED "ROYAL
ROOSTER," *FAR RIGHT,* CELEBRATES
THE HARBINGER OF DAWN IN THE
TRADITIONAL STYLE OF POLISH
FOLK ART. TEARDROPS
"ROMANZA," *NEAR RIGHT,* AND
"FLEUR DE PROVENCE," *BELOW
RIGHT,* REVEAL THE POLES' ADMI-
RATION FOR FRENCH CULTURE AS
WELL AS THEIR OWN SKILL IN
PAINTED DETAIL.

By 1867, a newly constructed gasworks provided the technology that allowed glassblowers to control the intensity of a flame, making it possible to create large, thin-walled glass globes, and the Christmas ornament industry was launched.

To call it an industry is somewhat misleading, as it is more properly a cottage industry: Entire families often worked out of their homes. Usually the father would blow the glass and the mother would decorate it. Even young children got into the act, painting simple designs, applying glitter, and packing the ornaments in boxes. Thousands of German ornament molds were created in the period from 1870 to 1930. Many molds were replicated in several sizes, and because so many have been lost, it is impossible to know how many designs there were, although it is estimated that there were at least five thousand different styles. Some of the most popular molds were Santas, pinecones, fruits, birds, and other animals. Lauscha became a leader in this craft, producing many of the blown-glass ornaments sold in the United States from the 1870s until the start of World War II.

At first the German glass ornaments sold in the United States were available only at East Coast department stores. However, in 1890, F. W. Woolworth made the glittering beauties available nationwide through his chain of stores. Ironically, Mr. Woolworth was coerced into buying the first batch of ornaments on a buying trip to Philadelphia. The wholesaler agreed to refund his twenty-five-dollar investment if the baubles failed to sell. Woolworth sold out within a few days and the next year placed a much larger order, which also quickly disappeared from the shelves. The following year (1890), he made his first trip to Europe and bought directly from Lauscha jobbers.

With Woolworth's resounding success, other jobbers got in on the act.

Not all ornaments were made in Germany. As the gateway between Russia and Western Europe, Poland has absorbed the influences of many cultures in its thousand-year history. Poland's artisans learned the technique of glassmaking during the Renaissance. When Poland was occupied by Prussia and Austria in the eighteenth and nineteenth centuries, knowledge of various crafts was exchanged, and by the 1850s the Poles had adopted the Bohemian skill of blowing small hollow glass beads for jewelry, folk costumes, and elaborate headdresses. By the 1920s, Poles made large free-blown and elaborately painted glass balls,

A Brief History of Glass Ornaments

FLIGHTS OF
FANCY

Christopher
Radko's
Ornaments

teardrops, flask shapes, ovals, and twisted forms like icicles and parasols. They also perfected the art of inserting colorful reflectors into round balls (see "Reflected Glory," page 41) that rivaled in beauty those made in Germany.

Another supplier of nineteenth- and early twentieth-century ornaments was Bohemia, which specialized in beaded ornaments made from the same mouth-blown, hand-painted beads that served in costume jewelry and as dressmakers' decorations. Strung on wires, the beads were formed into simple shapes such as stars, snowflakes, stockings, and bells, as well as more elaborate three-dimensional baskets, sleds, boats, animals, and candelabra.

Another specialty was the delightful glass garlands of Santas, train cars, acorns, or other tiny figures interspersed with plain or faceted beads.

Although they were regarded as delightful trinkets, Christmas ornaments were made from scrap glass and weren't expected to last long. Inexpensive—many sold for just a nickel or a dime—they were considered replaceable and certainly not worthy of collectible status.

World War I interrupted, but did not end, the manufacture of glass ornaments. Poland was primarily occupied by German and Austrian forces, so any ornaments made during that time would have been labeled as German or Austrian, and most Polish ornaments produced before the 1930s were sold in Europe. World War II again put a stop to Polish exports to the United States, but the craft endured. In fact, some German companies brought their molds to occupied Poland, taking over Polish factories for the manufacture of their own ornaments. When the Germans hastily evacuated before the Russian army invaded at the war's end, they left behind many molds, some of which are still in use to this day.

After the war, Lauscha became part of East Germany. The Communist regime and changing fashions spelled the decline of the glass ornament industry as a whole. Many East German glassblowers and other craftsmen fled the Communist sector, relocating in West Germany or elsewhere, where they took up new occupations. Racked by war, relocation, and political turmoil, artisans let the old molds fall into disrepair; others were lost or misplaced in attics and basements. With the passage of generations, the molds that rep-resented the industry's creative wealth were forgotten. The art of ornament making did not fare much better in Poland or Czechoslovakia.

In the postwar years, machine-made spheres in bright colors began to be mass produced, but whimsical and wonderfully diverse painted figures were considered old-fashioned. In the United States families decorated their (often silvertoned aluminum) trees with glass balls in silver, gold, red, green, and cobalt blue, or with plastic and Styrofoam ornaments, all often made in Japan. By the early 1980s, the European art of blowing decorative glass ornaments was all but extinct. That sad state of affairs would change dramatically with the arrival on the scene of Christopher Radko, who would single-handedly revolutionize the Christmas ornament industry.

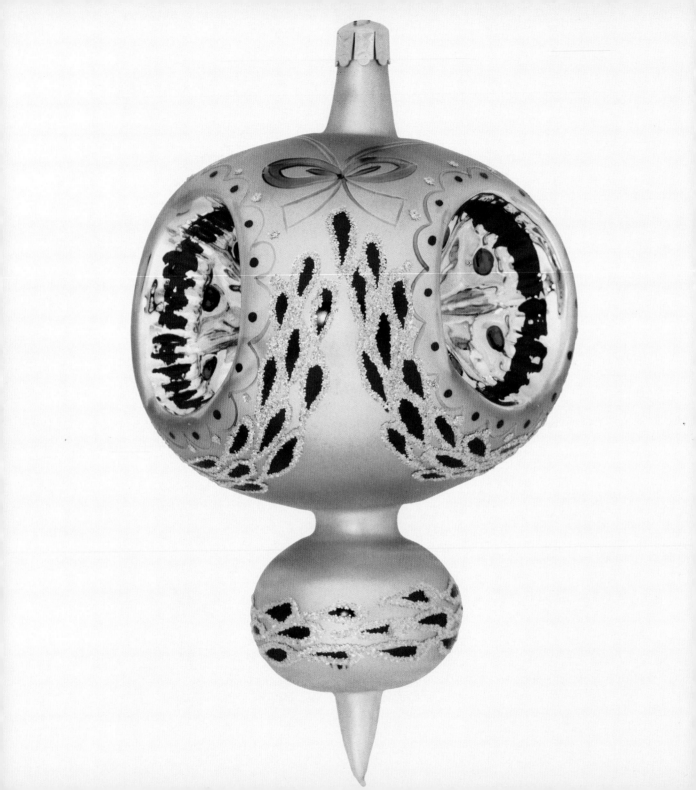

Chapter One

JUST

LIKE

GRANDMA'S

BELIEVE IN ANGELS

ANGELS ARE PERENNIALLY POPU-
LAR ORNAMENTS, WHETHER ON
THEIR OWN OR ATOP HEARTS,
STARS, OR BELLS. "CELESTIAL
HEARTS," *ABOVE,* "ANGELIQUE,"
RIGHT, AND "EVERY TIME A BELL
RINGS," *OPPOSITE BELOW,* ARE
EACH HANDBLOWN FROM TWO
SEPARATE MOLDS, THEN
ADORNED WITH EMBOSSED
GILDED CARDBOARD WINGS.
"MIDAS TOUCH," *PAGE 18,* IS A
CLASSIC POLISH REFLECTOR.

HRISTOPHER Radko's motto might well be that every cloud has a silver lining. Not just because his stunning Christmas ornaments are lined with luminous silver, but because he turned what was at first glance a holiday tragedy into a business that revived the European tradition of hand-made glass ornaments. The man is an optimist who firmly believes that, given sufficient time, it is entirely possible to find a needle in a haystack.

Christopher grew up in Scarsdale, New York, a suburb of New York City, the son of two doctors. In the Radko household, Christmas was a time of traditions, starting with elaborate decorations. Poinsettia plants, princess pine garlands, and wreaths of fragrant balsam filled the house. The Radko children helped their parents trim the tree, and as they grew up each took on more and more of the responsibility. All the decorations came out right after Thanksgiving, and the tree would go up the first week in December.

"It took four days to decorate the tree," recalls Christopher. An unchanging ritual was enjoyed year after year: "The first day we'd put up the tree, then we'd wait a day for the branches to settle and the tree to drink its water. Meanwhile, we'd be untangling last year's lights and making sure they all worked. Back in the 1960s, if one light went out, they all went out." Miniature lights didn't appear until the second half of the 1970s. "We had the large C-7 light bulbs in different colors, and bubble lights, too!" says Christopher. "I can remember when I first saw a purple bulb, but in boxes with four replacement bulbs only one was purple, so I'd go through all the replacement sets in the hardware store and take out just the purple bulbs and make full sets of purple and hope that the checkout person wouldn't notice."

Then all the lights would be placed on the tree. "I'd study the lights from a distance," says Christopher, "and let my eyes go blurry and see if there were too many of one color on any one part of the tree. Then I would go up and unscrew them and rearrange them so the colors were evenly distributed."

TWIST
AND TURN

"MERLIN SANTA," *FAR LEFT*, COM-
BINES A FREE-BLOWN ICICLE AND
SPHERE WITH A MOLDED HEAD.
"LONG ICICLE," *CENTER LEFT*, IS
FREE-BLOWN IN POLAND AND
DATES TO CHRISTOPHER'S FIRST
COLLECTION IN 1986. "CLOWN
SNAKE," *LEFT*, WAS INSPIRED BY
VICTORIAN DECORATIONS THAT
REPRESENT THE SERPENT IN THE
GARDEN OF EDEN, MADE MORE
APPEALING WITH CLOWN FACES.
THESE DELICATE ORNAMENTS
SHOULD BE USED AS ACCENTS AT
THE TIPS OF TREE BRANCHES.

IN PERFECT SHAPE

THIS PAGE, CLOCKWISE FROM TOP LEFT: "VICTORIAN STRAWBERRY" SUGGESTS THE ROMANTIC VIEW OF NATURE EMBRACED BY PRE-RAPHAELITE PAINTERS. "SCARLETT'S WEDDING DRESS," ORIGINALLY ISSUED IN WHITE, IS BASED ON THE MAPLE-LEAF PATTERN ON THE FICTIONAL SOUTHERN BELLE'S FIRST WEDDING GOWN. THE WIT-TILY NAMED "ENGLISH MUM" RECALLS FINE EMBROIDERY. CHRISTOPHER'S FASCINATION WITH THE GLITTERING NIGHTTIME SKY IS EXPRESSED IN "CELESTIAL." "MEDITERRANEAN SUNSHINE" CHEERFULLY RECALLS SUNNIER CLIMES. EXOTIC "SCHEHERAZADE," IN CITRUS COLORS AND GOLD GLITTER, EVOKES THE SILVER-TONGUED WIFE OF THE INDIAN SULTAN IN THE ARABIAN NIGHTS, WHOSE LIFE WAS SPARED THANKS TO THE TANTALIZING TALES SHE TOLD EACH NIGHT.

On the third day the Radkos would put the small ornaments on the top of the tree, using a tall ladder. Christopher and his sister had to sort out the ornaments, making sure that all the hangers were on tight. Then they would take turns standing on the ladder and passing up ornaments. "My sister had her favorite ornaments she'd hang up, and I had mine," he recalls. "We always rearranged each other's ornaments, trying to make room for our own favorites. 'Oh, you don't really like that one, I'll hang it deep inside,' we'd say."

Once the top of the tree was filled with ornaments, the person at the top of the ladder would place an angel, a star, or a finial at the very tip. Finally, tinsel was carefully applied and the ladder was removed. On the fourth and final day, the lower part of the tree would be similarly decorated with the larger ornaments and tinsel.

Christopher's paternal grandparents, who were born in Poland, and his maternal grandparents, who were French, all lived nearby, and

had for years accumulated traditional European glass Christmas ornaments, as had their parents before them. Christopher's parents had continued the tradition of collecting ornaments, and now Christopher and his brother and sister were the fourth generation to do so. "We had emotional connections to our ornaments," explains Christopher. "A lot of them dated from the turn of the century. Some of them were very simple, not necessarily very intricate or fancy. Many of their colors were all worn off or had deteriorated by the time I was on the scene. More important to us than the aesthetic of the ornament was the emotional connection. Certainly my mother remembers hanging ornaments as a child, and her mother before her, and so on."

Even as a teenager, Christopher had an intuitive understanding of the sentimental value of these fragile treasures. "I remember restoring some of our old ornaments—some of which were sixty or seventy years old. I would take glue and

LIFE'S A BALL

A SPHERE'S SIMPLICITY MAKES IT A PERFECT CANVAS FOR MYRIAD DECORATIVE STYLES. "THE HOLLY," *TOP*, IS A GRACEFUL RENDERING OF THE PLANT VENERATED BY DRUIDS FOR ITS ABILITY TO WARD OFF EVIL SPIRITS. ITS EVERGREEN LEAVES AND RED BERRIES WERE ADOPTED AS A SYMBOL OF CHRISTMAS, REPRESENTING EVER-LASTING LIFE. AFTER THIS ORNA-MENT IS HAND-PAINTED, THE BOLD COLORS ARE TRACED IN GOLD GLITTER. "DEEP SEA," *CEN-TER*, DEBUTED IN THE FIRST RADKO LINE AND WAS REISSUED IN 1995 TO CELEBRATE THE COM-PANY'S TEN-YEAR ANNIVERSARY. CHRISTOPHER'S LOVE OF ART DECO TURNS UP IN MANY ORNA-MENTS, INCLUDING "HARLEQUIN," *BOTTOM*. OTHER INCARNATIONS FEATURE PASTEL COLORS, BLACK AND WHITE, AND LARGER DIA-MONDS, WITH THE DIAMONDS ALWAYS ACCENTED WITH GLIT-TER. A COMPLEMENTARY PATTERN ALSO APPEARS ON A FOUR-SPHERE TREE TOPPER.

FOUND IN SPACE

THE INVENTION OF THE ZEPPELIN A CENTURY AGO MADE THE BULLET-SHAPED, GAS-FILLED AIRSHIPS A POPULAR SUBJECT FOR FREE-FORM BLOWN-GLASS ORNAMENTS. FASCINATED BY AIR TRAVEL SINCE CHILDHOOD, CHRISTOPHER INCLUDED THE R.A.F VARIATION IN "ZEPPELINS," AS PART OF HIS SECOND COLLECTION. BOTH IT AND "THE LOS ANGELES," WITH RIBBED SIDES INSPIRED BY A WORLD WAR I REPARATION DIRIGIBLE, ARE POLISH MADE AND HAVE ANNEALED HOOKS AND SPUN-GLASS TAILS TO SUGGEST EXHAUST. BRAND-NEW "ZIPPIDEE ZEPPELIN," *FAR LEFT*, MIXES HISTORY AND FANTASY. NOTE THE DIFFERENT TAIL AND ORNAMENT CAP TREATMENT.

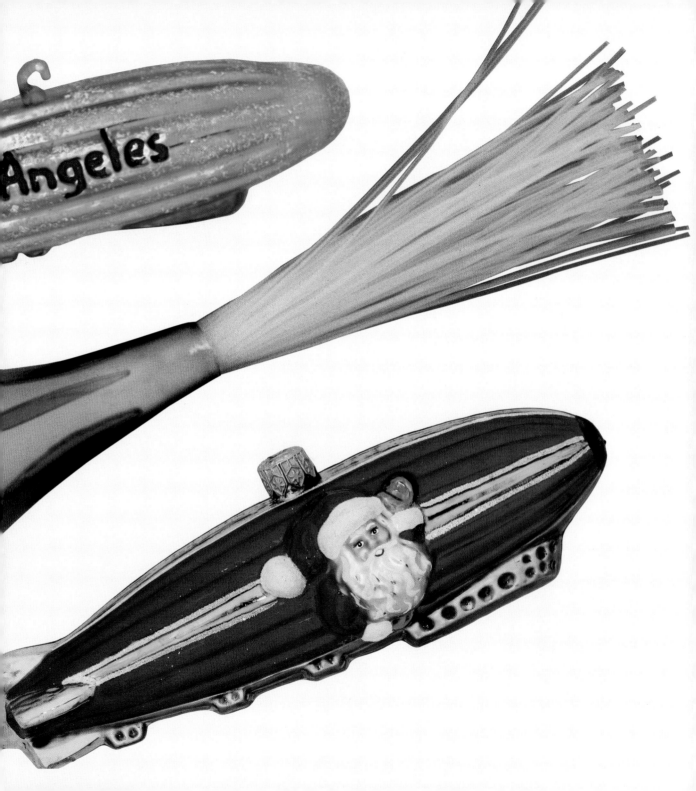

TREE-TRIMMING TIPS

THE MORE ORNAMENTS, THE MERRIER

As Christopher says, paraphrasing Mae West, "When it comes to Christmas, too much of a good thing can be wonderful." His style of tree-trimming is to load on the lights and ornaments until barely a sprig of greenery is in evidence. Here are his dos and don'ts to follow when decorating your own Christmas tree.

❋ **CHOOSE THE RIGHT TREE.** Douglas or Noble firs have sturdy, well-spaced branches, allowing you to tuck ornaments between them. Avoid Scotch pines, which have limp branches that don't support ornaments properly. The best-sized tree is one that is at least a foot taller than the tallest member of your family and at least a foot shorter than the ceiling, to allow room for a finial. If you use an artificial tree, select one with separate branches. Such trees will not flatten out when stored.

❋ **KEEP IT FRESH.** If you plan to keep the tree outdoors for a few days before setting it up, place it where it will not be exposed to the drying effects of wind and sun. If you bring it indoors, keep it away from radiators and hot-air vents. To further extend the life of your tree, just before setting it up, trim one inch

off the bottom. Be careful not to remove or cut off any of the bark, as this will sever the water-thirsty live wood below. Attach the tree stand immediately after cutting.

Give your tree at least a gallon of water, and replenish it daily. Use hot water to enhance circulation. For every quart of water, mix in 1 tablespoon liquid iron (available at garden supply stores); 2 tablespoons light corn syrup; and 1 tablespoon chlorine laundry bleach. Iron helps keep the tree green; corn syrup nourishes it; bleach fights bacteria and fungi.

If you plan to wait several days before trimming the tree, cut an inch off the bottom, place it in a bucket with the enriched water mixture, and keep it outside in a sheltered place or an unheated garage. Trim off another inch when you bring it inside.

❋ **USE A STURDY STAND.** Make sure your stand's size and weight are appropriate to the size of your tree. An excellent American-made, welded-steel stand—available in three sizes—comes from Sleighbells (800-809-8784).

❋ **WRAP THE TRUNK.** After you have attached the lights (See "The Light Fantastic" on page 66), a practical and attractive touch is to wrap the tree trunk with tinsel garland. Its reflective quality creates additional interior sparkle while hiding electrical cords.

✳ ATTACH THE TOPPER.
If you have trouble getting the finial or tree topper to stand straight, wrap the growing tip of the tree with aluminum foil so the finial will fit more securely. If the tip is too short to properly secure the finial, attach a wood dowel to the tip with wire to extend it.

✳ CHECK CAPS, SPRINGS, AND HOOKS.
Before you  hang a single ornament, check that the copper cap, or crown, at the top is snugly attached by the spring loop inside. If the loop is loose, pull it out, leaving the cap on the ornament. Reshape the circle at the top, then stretch open the spring like a wishbone. Pinch it closed and reinsert in the crown. It should now grip the ornament firmly.

Ornament hangers should have long loops at both ends to secure both the ornament cap and the tree branch. Small hooks can all too easily slip off a branch, particularly if it starts to droop. For larger ornaments, cut very thin green florist's wire into strips about six inches long. Wrap one end through the spring hook at the top of the ornament, making a loop about two inches long. Then wrap the other end of the wire around the branch a few times in a corkscrew motion. Be careful not to overlap the wire; spread it out so that later it can be pulled off the branch without having to unwind it. Wire can scratch ornaments, so be careful when using it. For this reason, ornaments should never be stored with wires or hooks attached.

✳ ORNAMENT TIME.
Decorate the top of your tree first to avoid brushing against and scratching lower ornaments. Use a sturdy ladder if the tree is over seven feet tall. Depending on the height of your tree, you may be on the ladder for half the project, so it is a good idea to have a helper. Work around the tree, placing the largest and favorite ornaments where they will be most visible. Usually, you'll want to place smaller ornaments near the top of the tree and larger ones below. Clip-on ornaments work well at the top of the tree. Hang shiny globes inside the branches for a full look.

✳ LAYER ON THE GARLANDS.
Lay the center of the strand of glass beads on the tip of a branch, then attach the remaining ends inside the tree on either side of the branch, forming a scallop shape. Or swag garlands from one outer branch to another in a series of U shapes. Radko garlands have a small hook on either end, but an ornament hook or twist of florist's wire adds a measure of security. Likewise, the center portion of longer garlands can be wired to the tree.

✳ THE SPARKLE OF TINSEL.
If you choose, add strands of tinsel to branch tips in imitation of real icicles. To ensure a natural look, be sure that each cluster of tinsel hangs perfectly vertical and doesn't touch any of the branches below.

✳ THE FINAL TOUCH.
A fabric skirt beneath the tree will hide the stand and electrical cords.

FOLLOW
YOUR STAR

THE SYMBOL OF CHRISTOPHER'S COMPANY, THE STAR MAKES FREQUENT APPEARANCES. MADE OF INDIVIDUALLY BLOWN GLASS BEADS WIRED TOGETHER WITH STURDY FILAMENT, THESE GRACEFUL ORNAMENTS ARE MADE IN THE CZECH REPUBLIC, MUCH AS TINY FACETED GLASS BEADS WERE CRAFTED FOR PERSONAL ADORNMENT 200 YEARS AGO. SEVERAL OF THE FIVE JEWEL-TONE STARS, VARIATIONS OF "FIRST SNOW" AND "RAINBOW SNOW," SHOW HOW DIFFERENT COLOR COMBINATIONS CAN CREATED MYRIAD EFFECTS. THE SIX-POINT RED, GREEN, AND SILVER STAR, FROM THE "CHRISTMAS CONSTELLATIONS" SERIES, CONTAINS MORE THAN 50 INDIVIDUAL BEADS; ITS ALL-SILVER COMPANION HAS EVEN MORE.

Christopher Radko's Ornaments

retrace where the glitter had all rubbed off and put fresh glitter on. If an ornament was broken I would mend it. It was like putting together a jigsaw puzzle. I would apply tissue paper on the back and then glue it to create a framework on the inside of the ornament. I was usually pretty good at mending ornaments and then covering over the repaired part with glitter so that from a distance you wouldn't ever know it was broken."

Every year, Christopher's family would make a pilgrimage into Manhattan shortly after Thanksgiving. There they would gaze at the Christmas tree at Rockefeller Center and stand enthralled in front of the intricate holiday window displays at Saks Fifth Avenue, Lord & Taylor, Macy's, B. Altman's, and other department stores. Finally, they would purchase a dozen or so new ornaments to add to their tree, each child selecting some of the baubles, which, although made of glass, reflected more modern designs than most in the family collection.

Another family expedition involved the selection and purchase of a live Christmas tree, which was always fresh and stood well over twelve feet tall to fit the family's cathedral-ceilinged living room. Sometimes a smaller live tree would stand in the dining room, and Christopher often had a small artificial one in his bedroom. By the time he was sixteen and could drive, the job of selecting a Christmas tree had fallen to Christopher, who delighted in this responsibility. What he did not enjoy was having to scrub the hardened sap from the previous year's tree off the rusted old-fashioned, cast-iron tree stand before setting up the new tree.

Meanwhile, Christopher attended Columbia University, remaining in New York City after graduation. The Christmas of 1983, when he was in his early twenties and home from Manhattan for the holidays, Christopher made a minor decision that wound up profoundly changing his life: He purchased a shiny red and green aluminum Christmas-tree stand to replace the old one. He installed the tree and over the next few days he and his sister decorated it with more than a thousand handmade, mouth-blown ornaments, as they had done for years.

The very next morning disaster struck! The new stand, while clean and

A FULL WEEK'S WORK

CRAFTSMANSHIP FROM START TO FINISH

THE BIBLE tells us that it took God seven days to create the world, and it takes no less to create just one of Christopher Radko's exquisite handblown ornaments. Here is a day-by-day look at the process.

DAY 1: A glassblower blows the ornament and tempers it in a second firing.

DAY 2: A silversmith coats the interior of the ornament with a solution of silver nitrate, then plunges it into hot water to hasten the chemical reaction. The ornament is then given a soapy bath and left to dry upside down overnight.

DAY 3: Ornaments are gently cleaned with a soft cloth, hand-coated with a base of matte lacquer, and left to dry overnight. The lacquer may be white for a snowman, red for a Santa.

DAY 4: An artist applies an overall design using a variety of both shiny and matte colored lacquers.

DAY 5: Other artists add such details as tiny snowflakes, the blush on Santa's cheeks, seeds on strawberries or watermelons, or the eyelashes on an angel.

DAY 6: Glitter, diamond dust, or perlini beads are meticulously applied to highlight certain details on the ornament.

DAY 7: The long glass stem, known as the pike, is snipped off, and a metal cap is attached to hold the spring loop. A tag that describes the manufacturing process is also attached. The ornament is now ready to be gently packed and sent on its way.

BUILDING TRADITIONS

ONE OF A SERIES OF CHAPELS, "MIDNIGHT MASS," *LEFT*, WEARS A GENEROUS MANTLE OF GLITTER-ING "SNOW" ON ITS STEEPLY PITCHED ROOF AND AT ITS BASE. A SWISS CROSS OVER THE DOORS IDENTIFIES THE LOCALE. THE CHURCH SEEMS TO GLOW FROM WITHIN, THANKS TO THE STAINED-GLASS WINDOWS CREATED WITH JEWEL-TONE LACQUERS.

❋

CRUNCH TIME

"NUTCRACKER CRUNCH," *OPPO-SITE*, IS ONE OF NUMEROUS NUT-CRACKER ORNAMENTS. WITH TYPI-CAL RADKO WORDPLAY, THE NAME ALLUDES TO THE FIGURE'S COMPRESSED SHAPE AS WELL AS HIS FUNCTION. HIS PIERCING GAZE, WELL-ARTICULATED HAIR AND BEARD, AND GLITTER-COVERED EYEBROWS AND MOUS-TACHE GIVE HIM A DISTINCTION BELYING HIS SQUAT STATURE. CRUNCH IS DRESSED TO THE NINES IN A BRASS-BUTTONED UNIFORM, COMPLETE WITH EPAULETS AND CAP.

SHIMMY
AND
SHIMMER

IN THE TRADITION OF CZECH
BEADED ORNAMENTS, ONE OF
THREE "BIG WIGGLES," *ABOVE,* IS
MADE OF SMOOTH AND FACETED
PIECES OF GLASS. A SYMBOL OF
VANITY, PEACOCKS ARE
NONETHELESS MAGNIFICENT. IN
THE CASE OF "PROUD PEACOCK,"
RIGHT, THE MOLDED REGAL BIRD
STRIKES AN APPROPRIATE POSE
ON A FREE-BLOWN GLOBE COM-
PLETELY COVERED WITH ROYAL
BLUE GLITTER.

trim, simply was not strong enough to support the weight of a fourteen-foot tree laden with lights and hundreds of ornaments. In one terrible moment the treasured glass globes, reflectors, icicles, pinecones, Santa Clauses, stars and comets, snowmen, angels, birds, and other glass ornaments the family had been collecting for more than half a century were dashed to the floor, almost all of them shattering instantly. Of course, Christopher was filled with remorse. The Grinch had definitely stolen Christmas, or, as his Polish grandmother said, "Chris has ruined Christmas. What will we do?" Needless to say, it was not the happiest holiday ever celebrated in the Radko household.

It was a multigenerational loss, and not just the ornaments were gone. "With sudden and resounding finality, it seemed that the door that linked me and my family to the memories of Christmases past had slammed shut," recalls Christopher. "We were devastated."

In the months that followed, Christopher embarked on a quest to replace the heirloom ornaments that had been destroyed. But instead of handmade ornaments, he found only flimsy, mass-produced objects, many made of plastic or Styrofoam, and often manufactured in countries that had no tradition of celebrating Christmas. Those trinkets lacked the delicacy and magic of glass creations; more important, they were deficient in

MULTIPLE EXPOSURES

"VICTORIAN SANTA BALLOON," *FAR LEFT*, COMBINES ANGEL HAIR, CHROMOLITHOGRAPHY, METALLIC RIBBON, AND CRINKLY GOLD WIRE TO REPLICATE ORNAMENTS CRAFTED OVER A CENTURY AGO. MATTE AND SHINY WHITE LACQUER CREATE A SATINY HARLEQUIN PATTERN ON ITS TWO GLOBES. MADE FROM TWO MOLDS, "BAVARIAN SANTA," *LEFT*, CARRIES A SMALL UNADORNED EVERGREEN, A TYPICALLY GERMAN IMAGE. THE TOUR DE FORCE "SUGAR CONE," *ABOVE*, FEATURES TWO BIRDS FLUTTERING BESIDE THE RAINBOW-HUED PINECONE TO WHICH THEY ARE JOINED WITH SMALL SPRINGS.

what Christopher calls the "heart of Christmas."

The following Easter, Christopher visited relatives in Poland. Still haunted by the loss of the family decorations, Christopher searched for glass ornaments, but found none. Then he took a different tack, asking whether anyone was still practicing the art of blowing ornaments. There were some glassblowers who did make ornaments, it turned out, but not at that time of year. Finally, he was introduced to a retired glassblower who agreed to make some ornaments for him. Christopher, who until then had not regarded himself as an artist, was invited to sketch some drawings of the traditional ornaments he sought.

His mission accomplished, Christopher returned to the United States with several dozen free-blown ornaments in traditional shapes—globes, reflectors, and icicles—delighted that he would be able to provide a pleasant surprise for his grandmother when Christmas rolled around. When he showed some of his friends the charming ornaments, they immediately wanted to buy them. Realizing he still had plenty of time to order more ornaments in time for Christmas, Christopher gladly sold the first batch, thinking this was an excellent way to supplement his meager income working in the mailroom of a talent agency. Over the next few months, via phone and telex, he commissioned more ornaments.

It was during this time that Christopher realized that he might have the germ of a business. To fill Christopher's orders, the original glassblower asked a few of his associates to help with production, and Christopher's way of working with this first small band of Polish glassblowers set the stage for the philosophy he continues to adhere to today: He respects the traditional ways of doing things, but encourages contemporary innovations that achieve similar effects with higher quality or greater efficiency. He honors the individual craftsmen, but is unrelenting in pushing them to achieve technical and aesthetic innovations. "No sooner do they achieve one goal than I raise the bar," he acknowledges, comparing himself to an athletic coach. "But I always appeal to their pride in craftsmanship. I know their art comes from the heart, and they know I appreciate that."

In the first years, communication was not always smooth. Christopher might ask for red pinecones, only to have blue ones arrive because the glassblower ran out of red paint. Timeliness was also a problem. After decades of working in a Communist regime, the idea that a shipment had to be in a certain place no later than the date promised was a foreign concept. Consistency was another

A SYMBOL OF GLAD TIDINGS, BELL ORNAMENTS HAVE LONG BEEN POPULAR. BOTH THE PINECONE ATOP A HOLLY-BEDECKED BELL AND THE OWL PERCHED ON A BELL EMBELLISHED WITH ACORNS AND OAK LEAVES, *OPPOSITE*, A PAIR CALLED "FOREST BELLS," ARE EXAMPLES OF TRADITIONAL GERMAN ORNAMENTS, EACH BLOWN FROM TWO MOLDS. A TINY GLASS CLAPPER HANGS FROM EACH. BETWEEN THEM ARE ONE OF THE SIX FREE-BLOWN "JUMBO TIFFANY BELLS" AND ONE OF A SERIES CALLED "PINE CONE BELLS." "CHERUB BELL," *ABOVE LEFT*, COMBINES THE FACE OF AN ANGEL WITH A BELL THAT DISPLAYS INTRICATE PAINTED DETAIL. IN ADDITION TO BELLS, TRUMPETS WERE EARLY FIGURAL SHAPES, WHICH OFTEN HAD A SLIVER OF METAL INSERTED SO THAT THEY COULD ACTUALLY TOOT. "TRUMPET PLAYER," *BELOW LEFT*, IS A POLISH ORNAMENT INSPIRED BY A TURN-OF-THE-CENTURY GERMAN VERSION.

MISSION POSSIBLE

"MISSION BALL," *NEAR RIGHT,*
RECALLS CHRISTOPHER'S PASSION
FOR LATE-NINETEENTH- AND
EARLY-TWENTIETH-CENTURY
DESIGN, HERE PAYING HOMAGE
TO THE REVIVAL OF MOORISH
ARCHITECTURE AND DECORA-
TION. "CRESCENT MOON SANTA,"
CENTER TOP RIGHT, LETS SANTA
DO A STAR TURN AS THE MAN IN
THE MOON. THE HAND-PAINTING
IS ACCENTED WITH GLITTER.

❄

YOU GOTTA LOVE HER

BROUGHT UP ON *I LOVE LUCY* RE-
RUNS, CHRISTOPHER COMMEMO-
RATES A SCENE IN WHICH THE
RED-HAIRED COMEDIENNE
SHOWS HUSBAND RICKY AN
ORNAMENT, SAYING, "LOOK AT
THIS, HONEY. WE'VE HAD IT EVER
SINCE WE'VE BEEN MARRIED. IT'S
MY FAVORITE." THE TEARDROP
ORNAMENT, *RIGHT,* IS APPROPRI-
ATELY NAMED "BLUE LUCY."

*Christopher
Radko's
Ornaments*

problem.
Although each
ornament is truly
unique, a specific-sized icicle cannot vary from three to five
inches; they all must be four inches
long. Christopher pushed the first five
Polish glassblowers to make their details
sharper and thus enhance the quality of
each ornament. As the number of people making ornaments for Christopher's
importing company grew, the message
of high quality, fine detail, and unique-
ness became synonymous with a Christopher Radko ornament.

Not one to rush into anything,
Christopher remained at the talent
agency for another two years. On vaca-
tions he would go to Poland and work
with the glassblowers to create new
designs. On weekends and lunch hours
he showed samples of his collection to
local store buyers. By his second year
he had sold seventy-five thousand dollars' worth of ornaments, more than
four times his salary. With no mentor,
Christopher had to teach himself,
through trial and error, all about
importing, shipping, customs regu-
lations, selling, warehousing, and,
finally, getting paid by customers.
When he made the break and went into

SOMETHING
IN THE AIR

"CHERRY BLOSSOMS," *ABOVE*, IS A
HARBINGER OF SPRING, MUCH AS
GREENERY AT CHRISTMAS HAS
ALWAYS BEEN USED. THIS DELI-
CATELY PAINTED ORNAMENT WAS
IN CHRISTOPHER'S FIRST COLLEC-
TION. DATING FROM 1988, THE
HOT-AIR "STRIPED BALLOON,"
LEFT, HAS A SILKY FINISH
ACHIEVED BY THE CONTRAST OF
MATTE WHITE AND GLOSSY
GREEN AND RED LACQUER, AND
IS ACCENTED WITH DELICATE
GOLDEN RINGS OF GLITTER.

FREE-FORM FANCIES

business full-time, the pessimists of the world assured him he would fall on his face. "No one will buy individual glass ornaments," he was told by old-timers in the business. But Christopher forged ahead, setting up his import business out of his family's basement and garage. He would pile boxes of ornaments into his 1982 Oldsmobile and drive around to stores himself. The early quarters and delivery method may have been primitive, but the ornaments spoke for themselves. The business grew by leaps and bounds. In 1999, more than three million ornaments were produced.

Compared to the elaborate creations he designs today, Christopher's early ornaments were simple and traditional in style. In fact, many of them were just like the treasures that had smashed on the floor a few days before Christmas at the Radko house. His earlier collections of blown-glass ornaments also were smaller than most of his present-day creations. The debut collection in 1986 included hand-painted spheres, icicles, bells, parasols, mushrooms, flasks, canes, and, of course, reflectors. Charming in shape and beautifully painted, they were a breath of fresh air in the predominantly tacky world of plastic and Styrofoam ornaments. Six years later, among the year's collection of over two hundred ornaments, Christopher designed a series of six painted reflectors entitled "Just Like Grandma's" to honor his Polish grandmother and the ornaments that had led to his business. No wonder he can rightfully say, "I've carried the torch since then."

AS LOVELY AS A TREE

NATURALISTIC RENDERINGS OF NATURE'S GIFTS HAVE LONG BEEN FAVORED AS ORNAMENT SUBJECTS. ONE FROM A SET OF "AUTUMN JEWELS," *FAR LEFT*, THIS BEAUTIFULLY VEINED LEAF IS MOLD-BLOWN IN POLAND. ALTHOUGH THE SHAPE LOOKS COMPLEX, "WINTER TREE," *LEFT*, IS ALSO BLOWN FREE-FORM BY A MASTER POLISH CRAFTSMAN, THEN PAINTED AND DUSTED WITH GLITTER.

❄

NEW WORLD MEETS OLD

THE MOTIF OF "PENNSYLVANIA DUTCH," *OPPOSITE LEFT*, IS INSPIRED BY THE DECORATION THAT EMBELLISHED FRAKTURS, WHICH WERE USED TO COMMEMORATE MARRIAGES AND BIRTHS, A GERMAN CUSTOM BROUGHT TO AMERICA.

REFLECTED GLORY

INDENTS CREATE DAZZLING EFFECTS

EFITTING their magical, light-enhancing qualities, reflectors go by many names, variously known as "eye-catchers," "indents," and "witch's eyes." The best, most dazzling reflectors have traditionally come from Poland. Not only are they beautiful and mysterious in their own right, but reflectors have the ability to act as prisms, reflecting back the beauty of other ornaments and the sparkle of electric lights—as they once did with candlelight. The Radko family tree that came crashing to the ground was ablaze with reflectors.

There are two basic ways to make reflectors:

✻ The more traditional procedure is to blow a ball or a teardrop shape, then put one side back in the fire to make it red-hot. Using a piece of charcoal shaped like a pencil, the glass-blower makes a small indent in the molten glass. He then carefully draws in a small breath, which makes the glass collapse around the dimple, creating a pleated shape.

✻ Less commonly a mold may be used to imprint a shape in the red-hot glass. The shape may depict a star, a flower, or even a scene such as the Nativity. With this technique, there is no need for the craftsman to intake breath.

No matter which procedure is used, the artisan must be very careful to align the indented area with the shape of the ornament. He or she must also maintain a sharply defined indentation to create a high-quality reflector. A single ornament may have several indents. (Reflectors may also be paired with mold-blown forms, as in the case of the Santa ornament on the opposite page.) Paint enhances the optical effect of the indent. Some reflectors are painted in a single color, others in stripes, or the star or petals of a flower may be picked out in different colors to highlight the ornament's prismatic effect.

Chapter Two

CREATING
NEW
TRADITIONS

FOUNDING FATHER

"PHILADELPHIA STORY," *ABOVE,*
DEPICTS BENJAMIN FRANKLIN
ATOP THE LIBERTY BELL,
COMPLETE WITH PATINATED
FINISH AND JAGGED CRACK. HE
HOLDS A KITE, THE STRING OF
WHICH WRAPS AROUND HIS
BUCKLED SHOES. TIED TO
THE STRING, AND VISIBLE ON
THE BACK, IS A TINY KEY LIKE THE
ONE HE USED TO CONDUCT
ELECTRICAL EXPERIMENTS
WITH LIGHTNING.

Christopher
Radko's
Ornaments

OURTEEN years after his pivotal trip to Poland, Christopher Radko has sold more than ten million of his marvelous ornaments, comprising more than five thousand designs. Some are increasingly complex variations of the traditional Polish free-blown styles he began with; many are intricate mold-blown shapes; still others are blown free-form, then adorned with delightful annealed glass details. In this diverse collection there is truly something for everyone, whether you are a dyed-in-the-wool traditionalist, your taste runs to the baroque, or you find perfection in simple shapes and exquisite craftsmanship.

Typically, over one thousand ornament designs are available at any one time. Old designs—fruits and vegetables, bells, icicles, reflectors, Santas, angels, and more, many virtually identical to those made a century ago—are perennial favorites. They have been joined by a whole new generation of glass creations never before seen on a Christmas tree. Some, like "One Small Step," acknowledge historical events; others, like "Miami Ice," a group of sartorially correct pastel snowmen, reflect popular culture. Still others, like "Carry a Torch," depicting the Statue of Liberty, celebrate American culture. Some, such as "Jubilation," an African-American Santa, honor cultural diversity.

Christopher finds inspiration everywhere. "The whole creative process comes easily," he says. "The concept usually just pops into my head. I could be walking down a street and see something and it just triggers an idea." When inspiration strikes, Christopher jots down a note or simply keeps an element in his mind until he gets home or back to his office. Then, he says, "All I have to do is to sit quietly and it's like a switch clicks on. It's almost like tuning in a radio signal; the ideas come and I'm off and running." The actual drawing doesn't come as easily. "I use a big eraser," he jokes. "Not being a classically trained artist, I have to constantly adjust and adjust and adjust until it gets right into position." A sense that he calls his "internal tuning fork" tells him when a design is just right. Today, Christopher works with a small staff of artists who render his ideas on paper and work with him until the tuning fork sings.

Christopher has always enjoyed visiting museums, a habit acquired as a

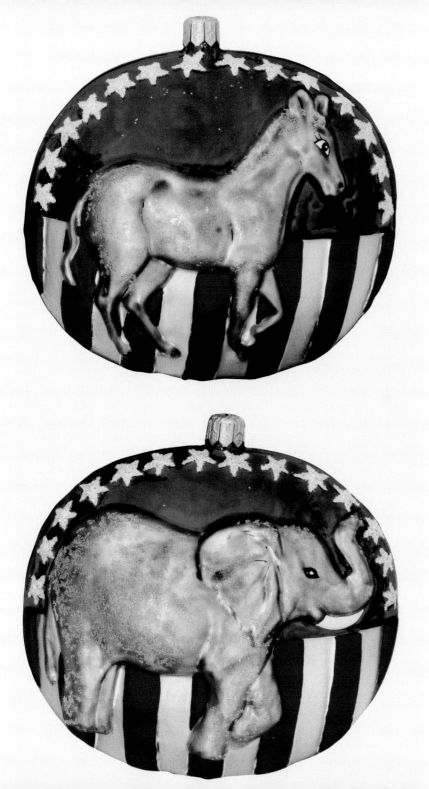

TWO-PARTY SYSTEM

WHETHER YOU'RE A DYED-IN-THE-WOOL DEMOCRAT OR A RESOLUTE REPUBLICAN, THERE'S AN ORNAMENT THAT EXPRESSES YOUR POLITICAL OPINIONS, SPECIFICALLY "DEMS DA ONES," *ABOVE LEFT*, AND "IT'S A PARTY," *BELOW LEFT*. THE WELL-MOLDED ANIMAL SYMBOLS OF DONKEY AND ELEPHANT ARE DRAMATICALLY SET OFF WITH PATRIOTIC COLORS IN THE FORM OF STARS AND STRIPES. YOU CAN'T GET ANY MORE AMERICAN THAN THAT!

NILE STYLE

"CHEOPS," *RIGHT*, AND "ETERNAL MYSTERY," *OPPOSITE BELOW*, ARE NUMBERS TWO AND THREE IN A LIMITED EDITION OF 15,000 ORNAMENTS EACH IN THE EGYPTIAN SERIES. HIEROGLYPHICS ON BOTH THE SARCOPHAGUS AND THE SPHINX AND A SCARAB ON THE FOREHEAD OF THE FORMER ARE BUT A FEW OF THE INTRICATE DETAILS.

❋

EXOTIC JOURNEYS

IN ONE OF A SERIES OF THREE GLOBES CALLED "BABYLON," THE PROFILES OF TWO BEARDED MEN AGAINST A GOLD BACKGROUND, *CENTER*, SUGGEST THE MAGNIFICENT ANCIENT CULTURE. "SULTAN'S PRIDE," *OPPOSITE ABOVE*, REVEALS CHRISTOPHER'S ONGOING INTEREST IN THE EAST, WITH ITS OPPORTUNITY FOR ELABORATE ACCENTS AND RADIANT COLOR.

child when he frequented New York's Metropolitan Museum of Art, where he was particularly fascinated by the Egyptian Wing. So it is no surprise that such ornaments as "Hieroglyph," "Cheops," and the aptly named mummy "All Wrapped Up" were inspired by ancient Egypt. Another ancient civilization was the source for a trio of hand-painted spheres collectively titled "Babylon." Not long after he started his ornament business, Christopher saw a display of Native American pottery on a visit to the Metropolitan, which lead to "Mimbres," six stunning painted globes honoring an ancient Southwestern tribe. Christopher's pride in his Polish heritage is expressed in "Polish Folk Dancers" and a series of painted globes called "Polish Folk Art."

Opera, literature, film, and television prove the genesis for other ornaments. Acknowledging one of literature's most memorable heroines, "Scarlett's Wedding Dress" picks out in gold glitter on white ground the maple-leaf pattern of her first wedding dress. The ornament has been so popular that it is now offered in an array of jewel tones. "Shirley" is all blond, curly-haired innocence; "Lola Ginabridgida" appropriately sexy. Perhaps the influence of contemporary culture is most evident in the lines of Radko ornaments licensed by The Walt Disney Company, Warner Brothers, Harley-Davidson, and a host of other companies (see "License to Play" on page 70).

Although Christopher and Christmas are inextricably linked, it is not the only holiday celebrated in his precious glass creations. "Ornaments help create a sense of wonder," he notes. "I think we need to let that sense of wonder carry over, spill over into the rest of the year." Celebrating Valentine's Day are delightful figures of lovebirds, hearts, cupids, and roses. Easter weighs in with a convocation of charming bunnies, ducks, geese, chicks, and other birds, and flower-bedecked eggs as intricate as Fabergé enamels are a feast for the eyes. St. Patrick's Day strikes a different mood, with an assortment of leprechauns wearing the green, complete with shamrocks, pots of gold, pipes, and Celtic harps.

"By George," a bust of our first president, and similar ones of Jefferson, Lincoln, and Hamilton; elephants and donkeys representing our two main political parties; and "Betsy Ross," "Stars & Stripes," and other patriotically inspired ornaments are ideal decorations for the Fourth of July. Doing the first European settlers proud,

Thanksgiving decorations include Pilgrims and Native Americans and the foods with which they celebrated their joint feast: ears of corn, pumpkins, grapes, plus a handsome gobbler. Halloween, which ranks as Christopher's second-favorite holiday, has inspired a myriad of ornaments: scarecrows, jack-o'-lanterns, black cats and bats, witches and wizards, ghosts, and all manner of spooks and goblins.

A new line of Christopher Radko ornaments called "Holiday Hares" celebrates various holidays, including Mother's Day with "You're the Best Mom" and birthdays with "Hare's to a Happy Birthday." When wedding bells chime, romance is in the air with ornaments like "Every Bead of My Heart," "June Buggy," and "Promises to Keep." And with the births that follow, equally heartfelt blown-glass treasures celebrate the occasion in the form of storks, silver spoons, booties, babes in buntings, and alphabet blocks.

All these ornaments are equally at home on a Christmas tree or as gifts or decorations during their respective holidays. "The Spirit of Kwanzaa" ornament acknowledges the African-American festival. Several ornaments honor the Jewish faith, including "Simon's Driedel" and "New Traditions," a ball decorated

ANCIENT ECHOES

ANOTHER MYSTERIOUS CULTURE, THAT OF A SOUTHWESTERN AMERICAN TRIBE CALLED THE MIMBRES, INSPIRED THIS LIZARD DESIGN, *BELOW*, PART OF THE "MIMBRES II" SERIES, FROM CHRISTOPHER'S FIRST COLLECTION. IN 1987, "AMERICAN SOUTHWEST," FOLLOWED. (ON PAGE 42, ANOTHER ORNAMENT IN THIS SERIES FEATURES A HUNTER WEARING AN ANTLERED HEADDRESS.)

Creating New Traditions

EASTER-EGG BOUNTY

PART OF A LARGE LITTER OF
HOLIDAY HARES, THE BUNNY IN
"HOPPY EASTER," *ABOVE*, IS NECK-
DEEP IN RICHLY DECORATED
EGGS, PROVIDING A WONDERFUL
OPPORTUNITY FOR THE TYPE OF
ELABORATE PATTERN
CHRISTOPHER LOVES. THE PLAY-
FUL FACES OF PANSIES, ONE OF
SPRING'S FIRST BLOOMS, MAKE AN
EASTER BOUQUET IN "BORDER
BLOSSOMS," *RIGHT*. WITH ITS
BRIGHT COLORS AND GOLD TRIM,
THIS ORNAMENT IS SUGGESTIVE
OF A PRECIOUS PIECE OF
FABERGÉ ENAMEL.

*Christopher
Radko's
Ornaments*

with a menorah, Star of David, and other Hebrew symbols. Such innovative creations acknowledge that today the observance of Christmas transcends the strictly religious rituals of Christianity. "As a child, I was curious about Jewish customs and holidays," says Christopher. "In fact, I am very curious about the customs and heart-based philosophies of all the world's religions. Today, the practical keeping of Christmas must become more inclusive of our diverse community."

With new ornaments being made each year, it is inevitable that others must disappear. Once the coloration or another detail on a specific ornament changes, the prior version is "retired." Some may change from year to year. For example, "Jumbo," also known as "Elephant on a Ball," originally stood on a plain red sphere, which was followed by a series of pastel-colored balls. Now the large pachyderm stands on a more detailed red ball with a saddle, so it has been retired twice. Sometimes a character changes completely. Blown from the same mold, Cardinal Richelieu was improbably reincarnated as Mrs. Claus, thanks to different painted details. (See "Blue-Chip Investments," page 50, for more on retired ornaments.)

Christopher has not just completely redefined the vocabulary of subjects appropriate for ornaments; his shimmering works reflect technological advances as well. Ornaments are made of tempered glass, the same material used for laboratory glass and casserole dishes and other cookware. This superior glass can withstand changes in temperature and is stronger than the scrap glass, full of impurities, traditionally used for ornaments. In the old days, ornaments were considered trinkets, and were not expected to last very long.

Today, Christopher's ornaments are durable enough to become family heirlooms. Antique and old figural ornaments were typically no larger than four inches tall; in contrast, many Radko ornaments are in the eight- to nine-inch range, some reaching ten or eleven inches! (Coming full circle, in 1998 Christopher launched a special line of petite ornaments that are scaled-down versions of popular larger designs and recolorations of previous small styles.) Achieving such a scale is in itself an impressive feat, but many of the ornaments also display a complexity of design that has never been achieved before.

"Two molds are more demanding than one," he explains, referring to ornaments like "Celestial Hearts" or "Bavarian Santa," comprised of two distinct shapes. The artisan makes a bubble of glass at the end of a long tube, then takes turns heating and expanding the bubble by blowing into it, before shaping it in one mold. He then blows another bubble just beyond the first and repeats the process in the next mold. Other designs require a free-blown sphere, for example, upon which

SPECIAL DELIVERY

THE WORD PLAY IN THE NAME OF "BUNNY EGGSPRESS," *LEFT*, IS TYPI-CAL OF MANY RADKO ORNA-MENTS. AKIN TO SANTA MAKING HIS ROUNDS ("SCOOTING STAR" DEPICTS SANTA ON A SCOOTER), THE RABBIT CARRIES A BASKET FULL OF DECORATED EGGS, WHILE GIFTS FOR CHILDREN ARE CLUSTERED ON THE FOOTREST. THE SYMBOLIC CARROT AT THE FRONT OF THE SCOOTER SPURS THE BUSY BUNNY ON.

❄

HEARTS OF GOLD

"SPRING ROMANCE," *BELOW*, TWO OF A THREE-PIECE ASSORTMENT, LOOK FOR ALL THE WORLD LIKE CLOISONNÉ, IN WHICH DIFFERENT COLORS OF ENAMEL ARE SEPARATED BY THIN METAL BANDS. THE JEWEL-LIKE MOLDED-GLASS CREATIONS WOULD BE EQUALLY AT HOME ON DISPLAY AT CHRISTMAS, EASTER, VALENTINE'S DAY, MOTHER'S DAY, OR ANY OTHER DAY OF THE YEAR, FOR THAT MATTER.

BLUE-CHIP INVESTMENTS

RADKO ORNAMENTS GROW MORE
VALUABLE OVER THE YEARS

RETIRED" and "on vacation" may sound like notations in a personnel file, but in the world of Christopher Radko these terms have different meanings. Each year's collection of Radko designs includes some old, some new, and some recolored ornaments. Many ornaments are best-sellers and remain in the line for years. "Scarlett's Wedding Dress," "Harlequin," and "Clown Snakes," originating in 1987, 1988, and 1989 respectively, are just a few examples of perennially popular styles. But to make way for new models, some earlier creations go "on vacation," meaning they are not available that year but will return in future years. The charming "Peas on Earth," for example, is on crop rotation for 1999. Other ornaments are retired permanently. "Retired ornaments have made their case and done their good service," explains Christopher.

Ornaments are retired for a variety of reasons. Some, such as "Hooked on Classics," a set of busts of Mozart, *right,* Chopin, and Bach, are limited editions that usually sell out in one season. Often one design is retired to open up space for a similar one. "Union Jack," a balloon wrapped with crinkled golden wire was retired in 1997 after two years in the line; a similarly shaped but differently decorated "French Regency Balloon" went on vacation in 1999, when "Angelic Ascent" was introduced. It reiterates the shape and use of gold wire, but displays yet another painted design and the addition of angel hair.

When an ornament is retired, essentially the mold is broken. "In the case of free-form ornaments," says Christopher," a retired ornament would never be made in that same size again. But," he adds, "we could bring it back by making it bigger or smaller." In 1998, for example, a line of miniature ornaments based on earlier, larger figures debuted. Other times a certain color is retired, but the ornament continues to be made in other colors. "Blue Slim Pickins" is no longer made, but his more traditional red brother is still in the line.

Stephen Robba, whose collection of Christopher Radko ornaments numbers somewhere between 1,200 and 1,500 items ("I stopped counting when it got above a thousand," he jokes), is an expert on the secondary market in Radko ornaments as well as publisher of a newsletter on the subject. (For information on how to order, see page 136.) He explains that all Radko ornaments tend to hold their value, but that many factors affect the prices individual designs can command. As with all collectibles, the rarer the item, the more valuable it tends to be, meaning retired and limited edition ornaments inherently have an advantage. The first six ornaments from the "Twelve Days of Christmas" series are in great demand, but "Partridge in a Pear Tree," *above,* is the most desirable, selling for anywhere from $650 to $1,000. In this case and others, condition is a factor; signed ornaments command the higher end of the price spectrum, as does having the original box. Several Web sites and the on-line auction house eBay offer retired ornaments, but most transactions are handled privately.

According to Robba, certain colors are more valuable, usually the first coloration in a series. All the Russian Santas are popular, but retired "White Russian Santa" tends to command the highest price, in the $200 range. Rarity is a definite factor in price considerations. Certain ornaments are made in limited quantities with a particular coloration to sell at one store. They are usually in great demand from day one. In one of his appearances on *The Donny and Marie Show,* Christopher handed out a custom-made ornament to everyone in the audience. This piece, which was never part of the regular line, is highly collectible. Similarly, in 1996 when "Circus Seal," *below,* was introduced, the seal was mistakenly painted lime green. Christopher immediately had the color corrected to gray, and the few green seals that slipped through are the object of desire to collectors. An odd-ball design like "Sweet Madame," a large smiling face on a pear, sold for $50 originally. Retailers didn't twig to Madam's overblown charm and it was retired after one year. Again, because the supply is limited and the demand on the secondary market large, it now sells for $150 to $200.

With Christopher Radko ornaments commanding such prices, fakes have appeared, often blown by machine, instead of handmade as authentic ones are. To ascertain that the ornament you are considering is genuine, look for the following hallmarks of authenticity:

❋ Careful application of lacquers and precision in free-blown ornaments

❋ Careful painting. Fakes will display poor attention to the details, with perhaps an eye painted in a different place than where it is indicated on the mold.

❋ A Christopher Radko tag explaining how the ornament is made.

❋ The copper crown bearing the name RADKO on top.

RING IN
THE NEW

sits a figure made from a mold, again all blown from a single piece of glass, as in the case of "Hey Diddle Diddle" and "Proud Peacock."

Christopher's dazzling finials, some of which reach a staggering nineteen inches in height, require a highly skilled glassblower to blow two, three, or even four balls, one on top of another. "Only the most skilled craftsman can produce these finials," says Christopher. "He might handle no more than thirty in a day." (For more on Christopher's finials, see "To Top It All Off" on page 132.)

Another technical innovation is the use of water-based lacquers for decoration. The paints used originally by nineteenth- and early twentieth-century artisans who worked out of their homes were based on flour, gelatin, and other ingredients found in their kitchens. These ingredients go a long way toward explaining why the paint on so many old ornaments disintegrated or faded with time. In the 1950s, industrial lacquers full of noxious chemicals were used on mass-produced ornaments. Inhaling those fumes could cause severe illness. "I care about the glassblowers' health," says Christopher, explaining why all his paints are acrylic and water based. "They are more stable," he continues. "Just don't expose the ornaments to great heat or too much sunlight or they might fade, just like fabric or fine paper."

As important as these new manufac-

turing processes are, it is his new design ideas that have taken Christopher's ornaments to a level never before achieved. It is important to realize, however, that technological and design innovations are often entwined. For example, Christopher pushed the glassblowers to make bigger ornaments. When they succeeded, he then created even larger designs. Among his innovations is the simple upending of tree toppers, turning them into elaborate hanging ornaments. He also originated the concept of combining shiny and matte lacquers on one ornament. In the early years of his business, some ornaments were dusted with antique crushed crystal glitter that Christopher unearthed as unused stock in a warehouse. The crystal glitter had real gold and silver melted into it, which tarnish just as solid metal does over time, creating an antique look. Christopher has introduced new kinds of glitter, including iridescent glitter, mica, and microscopic glass pearls (called perlini) that create a frosted effect.

In another twist on an old idea, clip-on attachments, formerly reserved for birds, have been extended to tiny Santas, snowmen, angels, bird nests, and even a kitten emerging from a stocking. Clip-ons are a great way to fill in spaces above branches.

Most importantly, the intricacy of design in ornaments of all subjects, shapes, and sizes is astounding. A case

SWEET CHARITY

"DEAR TO MY HEART," *ABOVE,*
DEPICTS A GIRL IN A BAGGY
CLOWN SUIT WHOSE HEART IS IN
THE RIGHT PLACE, EVEN IF SHE IS
WEARING IT ON HER HAT INSTEAD
OF HER SLEEVE. SALES OF THE
ORNAMENT, INSPIRED BY A TURN-
OF-THE-NINETEENTH-
CENTURY GREETING CARD, BENE-
FIT GROUPS THAT HELP PEDIATRIC
CANCER PATIENTS. ANOTHER 1999
RADKO CHARITY ORNAMENT ALSO
BEARS A GIFT: PROFITS FROM
"CUBBY'S RAINBOW," *RIGHT,* GO TO
AIDS CHARITIES. THE BEAR'S MULTI-
COLOR SWEATER ALLUDES TO THE
RAINBOW FLAG OF GAY LIBERA-
TION, BUT HIS TRUE COLORS ARE
EVIDENT IN THE RED AIDS AWARE-
NESS RIBBON IN HIS CAP.

*Christopher
Radko's
Ornaments*

54

in point: "Scooting Star" depicts Santa on a scooter decorated with three tiny Christmas trees. A toy bear peeks from the pocket of Santa's star-studded red robe. Another teddy clings to the steering column. In a basket on Santa's back are wrapped presents and toys. Santa's hat is topped not with a predictable pom-pom, but with the ornament cap. At least ten different colors of paint, all precisely applied, give the piece its colorful charm.

Today, Christopher Radko ornaments are made in Poland, Germany, the Czech Republic, and Italy. When he says, "I have taken ornaments to new heights, both free-blown and figural," he is not exaggerating. He has played a major role in reshaping traditions formed over generations in the countries that produce his designs.

Christopher originally looked for ornaments in Poland because he had relatives there and knew that many of his grandmother's ornaments originated there. The Polish tradition was primarily one of free-blown glass balls, teardrop and flask shapes, ovals, and twisted forms like icicles and parasols, as well as the famous reflectors. With Christopher's arrival on the scene, the glassblowers were delighted to see a revival of interest in their craft. When after several years he asked them to start making mold-blown ornaments, they rose to the challenge and found mold makers who had been working in other crafts (the molding process is similar for any cast object).

Ironically, because the Poles had not traditionally made ornaments from molds, they had none of the resistance to Christopher's ideas—making larger ornaments, for example—that he encountered later in Germany, where molded ornaments had been made for generations. Today, Poland produces not only reflectors and other free-blown ornaments, but most of the large and intricate mold-blown figural ornaments for which Christopher is known. "In time, I revolutionized the ornament industry in Poland," he says in all modesty, immediately giving the artisans their due. "The craftsmen are producing exquisitely hard-to-make designs that look even better than the originals that inspired them."

Christopher had been importing Polish ornaments for several years when he attended the German Toy Fair in Nuremberg. There he saw a few of the small, finely detailed figural ornaments in which the Germans had traditionally specialized. The ornaments were usually no more than three or four inches high— you might find the occasional five-inch Santa—and the quality of the designs in the

old molds, which were made of fired ceramic, was superb. But by the 1980s, the molds of more familiar subjects, like a basic Santa or a pinecone, that had been used repeatedly, had lost significant detail.

These ornaments were still being sold as boxed sets primarily in five-and-ten-cent stores. In addition to the diminished detail in the molds, the quality of the painting had also declined. "The molds' details often weren't even highlighted or expressed in the painting process," notes Christopher. Often an animal or a angel was simply dipped in one color instead of calling out details in various colors. By the 1980s, sloppiness was also common; for example, a dab of paint indicating an eye might be carelessly misplaced on the nose.

Starting in 1989, Christopher began a twofold effort to revive the tradition of fine German craftsmanship. First, he worked with artisans, using the familiar molds, but encouraged them to highlight various intricate painted details, such as different colors of flowers in a basket, and to generally improve their precision. Today, there are some traditional designs sold by other sources that may momentarily appear similar to a Radko ornament, but the latter is more detailed in its shape and superior in its applied decoration. Christopher also unearthed some of the more detailed and formerly lost German molds that had not been used in decades, and they are once again delighting young and old alike with their intricacy. For example, although

Creating New Traditions

BLAST OFF

"ONE SMALL STEP," *NEAR RIGHT*, CELEBRATES NEIL ARMSTRONG'S PARADIGM-CHANGING MOMENT WHEN HE STEPPED ONTO THE MOON, SAYING, "ONE SMALL STEP FOR MAN; ONE GIANT LEAP FOR MANKIND." THE MOON'S CRATERS ARE DEPICTED WITH REFLECTOR INDENTS. THE ORIGINAL SPACE TRAVELER BLASTS OFF IN "ROCKET SANTA," *CENTER RIGHT*. LIKE THE ASTRONAUT, HE TOO IS ENCLOSED IN A CLEAR GLASS BUBBLE. SANTA'S TINY METAL SPECS, COTTON-WOOL BEARD, AND "FUR"-TRIMMED CAP ARE DELIGHTFUL DETAILS. "SUPER SONIC SANTA," *BELOW RIGHT*, IN A NEEDLE-NOSED ROCKET, IS NOT ABOUT TO BE LEFT OUT OF THE FUN. THE DATE OF 2096 ON HIS SPACECRAFT IS EXACTLY ONE HUNDRED YEARS AFTER HIS ISSUE.

only a few inches tall, "Madeline's Puppy" and "Patrick's Bunny" display remarkable detail in the children's poses, costumes, and even their expressions. (Sadly, many other molds had been broken up and used as the rubble foundation for the autobahn and other roads after World War II.) According to Christopher, the skill of the old German mold makers is unparalleled, even today. "If I could go back in time," he says, "I would love to work with some of those master carvers."

In general, Christopher has built upon the glassblowing tradition of each country, then pushed the artisans to take their skills to greater and greater heights.

Thus he relies on artisans in the Czech Republic to make the traditional Bohemian glass bead garlands. The beads are still blown in the original molds made of bronze, which holds details such as jewel-like faceting beautifully; newer designs incorporating larger beads are made in Poland from aluminum molds. The Czechs traditionally created ornaments by wiring the beads into stars, sleds, boats, and other playful shapes. In his signature fashion, Christopher has continued and adapted this tradition to his own creative impulses. Among the most charming bead ornaments are those in a series of figures that includes "Big Wiggles," "Starman," and "Rudy Baby."

OUT OF THIS WORLD

MAN'S BEST FRIEND GETS TO GO EVERYWHERE HIS MASTER DOES AND "ASTROPUP," *LEFT,* IS NO EXCEPTION. THE PORTLY PUP SPORTS A GLASS BUBBLE HELMET AND A BREATHING PACK COVERED IN GLITTER AND ATTACHED WITH SILVER-COLORED CORDING. IN "SKY RANGER," *ABOVE,* CREATED IN A TWO-STEP PROCESS, SANTA WAVES AS HE TAKES OFF FROM THE NORTH POLE. THE ORNAMENT CROWN IS INTEGRAL TO THE ROCKET'S CONE.

FIRST AMERICANS

Until the 1950s, decorating a Christ-mas tree was not a custom in Italy, nor, for that matter, in most of Southern Europe, where the iconography cen-tered instead on the Nativity crèche. As a result, making Christmas orna-ments was not an entrenched custom; however, Italy does have a long tradi-tion of superb glassblowing. After World War II, some German ornament manufacturers relocated to Italy, and rather than try to compete with the German molded ornaments, focused on whimsical free-blown glass shapes.

Unlike the Polish free-blown orna-ments, which are mostly geometric shapes, most of the Italian subjects were fantasy figures of people and animals. Details such as arms and legs were annealed: First, using tempered glass, the glassblower makes the hollow body; then he heats a separate rod of glass and carefully adds details such as a foot, an arm, a tail, or an elephant's trunk. The juncture is heated to a high temperature and air is blown into the new piece of glass, making a hollow leg, for example, that is permanently attached to the main body. The artisan repeats the process until all the arms, legs, and other fea-tures are complete.

Today, many annealed ornaments are not silvered because of the difficulty get-ting the silver nitrate into all the nooks and crannies and (even more difficult) get-ting out the excess. Still, Christopher does have some of his creations silvered as ornaments were forty years ago if it significantly adds to their beauty.

During the last few decades prior to Christopher's working with artisans in Italy, Italian ornaments had become debased. A figure's arms might appear as just an undifferentiated tube of glass with a needlelike point at the end where the glassblower had twisted it off. Christopher suggested that the glassblowers add mittenlike hands and shape the anatomy of the arms and legs to make the thigh plumper than the ankle and the forearm thicker than the wrist. "Before, the figures looked like the cardboard rolls inside paper tow-els," he says. "I suggested they give them defined waists and developed chests, with the result that the ornament bodies are much shapelier." He also insisted that the interiors be hand-silvered and that bright, clean colors be used. "The European palette tends more toward subtle and darker earth-toned colors, which don't sell well in the United States," Christopher notes. The delightful Italian ornaments often are decorated with scraps of fabric, feathers, and spun glass.

A completely original concept is that of making certain designs in limited editions. Celebrating the business's ten-year anniversary, "On Top of the World" shows Santa sitting on a globe checking his gift list one last time. "The Twelve Days of Christmas," the first in a series of limited-edition ornaments, debuted in 1993 (see "Blue-Chip Investments," pages 50–51). Two years later Christopher began to offer sets of limited editions. For example, the series "Homes for the Holidays," issued in 1997 in an edition of ten thousand, includes three ornaments depicting gingerbread versions of Old World houses called collectively "Sugar Hill." The following year, "Sugar Hill II" appeared as a set of three more fantastical dwellings. Other ornaments are offered exclusively to members of the Starlight Family Collectors made up of over thirty thousand Christopher Radko ornament collectors. (See page 136 for informa-

tion on how to become a club member.)

The extraordinary reception to Christopher's ornaments has made his business enormously successful. "I have worked extremely hard, but I have also been extremely fortunate," he acknowledges. To give back some of what he has been given, he has created certain ornaments whose profits are donated to causes he supports. "Purchasing one of these ornaments as a gift allows you to give in two ways," explains Christopher.

An angel full of hope and prayer, "On Wings of Hope," wears an AIDS awareness heart that carries a message to all who admire her. "Dear to My Heart" fights pediatric cancer, while "Felina's Heart," an elegant puss complete with a pink ribbon, does the same for breast cancer. Profits from a series of baby animals tucked into stockings goes directly to the Christopher Radko Foundation for Children, which runs a home for Polish orphans. "It is very rewarding to have Christmas ornaments make such a difference to many lives!" says Christopher. Sales of these ornaments and Christopher's other charitable efforts have raised more than three million dollars. In these heartwarming ornaments, beauty and compassion go hand in hand.

FREEDOM OF FAITH

"THE SPIRIT OF KWANZAA," LEFT, CELEBRATES THE AFRICAN-AMERICAN FESTIVAL THAT BEGINS ON DECEMBER 26. THE FIGURE IS DRESSED IN KENTE CLOTH AND CARRIES A KINARA, A CANDELABRA REPRESENTING THE SEVEN DAYS OF THE HOLIDAY. IN HIS OTHER HAND, HE HOLDS OFFERINGS THAT CELEBRATE A FRUITFUL HARVEST. "SIMON'S DREIDEL," ABOVE, HONORS THE JEWISH FESTIVAL OF HANUKKAH, WHEN THIS SPINNING TOY WITH HEBREW LETTERS IS TRADITIONALLY GIVEN TO CHILDREN.

Chapter Three

THROUGH THE
EYES OF A
CHILD

THREE'S A CROWD

"3 BLIND MICE," *ABOVE*, IS ONE IN A SERIES OF ACROBATIC TRIAD ORNAMENTS, INCLUDING PENGUINS, SNOWMEN, CLOWNS, FROGS, AND EVEN SANTAS. DRESSED TO THE NINES, THESE MICE ADD COLOR TO THE OFT-TOLD NURSERY RHYME. ON THE OTHER SIDE, THEIR THREE SKINNY TAILS BEAR EVIDENCE THAT THIS TIME THEY GOT AWAY FROM THE BUTCHER'S WIFE. SALES OF "UNITED WE STAND," *PAGE 60*, BENEFIT INTERNATIONAL CHILDREN'S CHARITIES.

Christopher Radko's Ornaments

HINGS are magical and infinite when you are a child," says Christopher. "I think it is only when you get older that you start thinking about limitations." Perhaps even more than his boundless imagination, Christopher's greatest gift is his ability to retain a childlike joy in life's wondrous variety and beauty. What makes his ornaments so remarkable is not just their beauty and detail, but their almost mystical power to convey the magic of childhood to all who see them. They also trigger shared memories, uniting us all—regardless of age—in the experiences of growing up in the United States. Who could encounter the bright yellow bus called "Field Trip" and not recall the first day of school, catching up with old friends and meeting new ones as you bounce along the road? In fact, one of Christopher's goals is for his ornaments and other creations to help other people experience the joy that is so natural in childhood but often becomes obscured by day-to-day adult concerns. "When people visit my showrooms, they say, 'Wow, this is like Disneyland,'" he says. "What they mean is that they have stepped into a place outside the daily grind of the world we occupy. Senses are heightened, colors are brighter, scents are stronger, feelings are more intense. I want Christmas to be that way."

Christopher's own childhood and the culture of childhood have inspired many of his ornaments. Characters from classic children's literature, Mother Goose nursery rhymes, television shows, and films are the mother lode from which he mines ideas. The toy soldiers

SITTING PRETTY

THIS ORNAMENT, APTLY NAMED "OFF THE WALL," *LEFT*, SHOWS POOR OLD HUMPTY-DUMPTY IN TRANSIT, AS HIS SURPRISED EXPRESSION MAKES CLEAR. FORTUNATELY, HE IS MADE OF STRONG TEMPERED GLASS. FREE-BLOWN BY ITALIAN CRAFTSMEN, HIS EGG-SHAPED BODY IS FORMED FIRST, THEN SEPARATE PIECES OF GLASS ARE ATTACHED AND BLOWN TO FORM ARMS AND LEGS. IT WOULD DO MOTHER GOOSE PROUD TO SEE THE BLISS-FUL DISH AND SPOON IN "ON THE RUN," *OPPOSITE*. THE ELABORATE ORNA-MENT IS ALSO MADE IN ITALY. AFTER THE DISH'S LIMBS HAVE BEEN ANNEALED TO ITS BODY, THE CRAFTSMAN ATTACHES THE SPOON. THE UNLIKELY LOVERS ARE THEN LACQUERED AND TRIMMED WITH GLITTER.

Through the Eyes of a Child

FANTASY TRIP

REPORTS THAT THIS HANDSOME TOY SOLDIER, *RIGHT*, IS A POR-TRAIT OF CHRISTOPHER ARE UNCONFIRMED, BUT IT IS CERTAIN THAT AS A CHILD HE LOVED THE CHRISTMAS EXTRAVAGANZA AT RADIO CITY MUSIC HALL, WHERE PERFORMERS DRESSED LIKE "KING'S GUARD" MARCHED IN UNISON. THE SOLDIER'S SMART UNIFORM IS ADORNED WITH BRASS "BUTTONS" AND SILVER "BRAID"; HIS GUN IS MADE OF GLASS AND PAPER. HAD HE LIVED TODAY, HANS CHRISTIAN ANDERSEN MIGHT HAVE ENVI-SIONED HIS FAMOUS CHARACTER AS "TEENAGE MERMAID," *CENTER*. WHY EVER GROW UP IF YOU CAN SOAR INTO THE AIR LIKE "FLY BOY," *FAR RIGHT*, HIS SLIPPERED FEET SKIMMING THE GROUND? HIS SUIT IS FITTED WITH LACE-UP TIES AND BELT; HIS CAP, WHICH MELDS INTO THE ORNAMENT CROWN, SPORTS A FEATHER.

Christopher Radko's Ornaments

he played with as a child reappear dressed in their crisp uniforms; charming creatures recall how we cuddled up each night with a favorite stuffed animal; Nutcracker Suite dancers twirl *en pointe;* clowns show off their silly noses.

Like legions of youngsters before and after him, Christopher grew up on Mother Goose tales before graduating to *Aesop's Fables,* the fairy tales of the Brothers Grimm, *Alice in Wonderland,* and *The Wizard of Oz.* Later yet, the works of Jules Verne and H. G. Wells joined the strong vein of fantasy that runs throughout his favorite books. In his first ornament collection, Christopher named a reflector "Emerald City," but the three decorated spheres in the 1987 series "Dream Alice" were the first ornaments that actually depicted characters from storybooks; "Mother Goose" appeared in 1990. In the years that followed they were joined by a cast of heroes and heroines familiar to all youngsters: "Puss in Boots," "Aladdin," Little Red Riding Hood (in "To Grandmother's House We Go"), "Hansel and Gretel," the "Little Prince," and a host of other creations inspired by classic childhood tales.

Every child loves a trip to the big top, and Christopher was no exception. When we view his balancing elephants, performing seals, and happy clowns, we immediately recall the suspension of reality that takes over in a three-ring circus. And the childhood fantasies of being a tightrope walker, a lion tamer, or a clown return anew, if only for a brief moment.

ALL DECKED OUT IN CHAPS, VEST, AND BANDANNA, WITH HIS HOLSTER AND COWBOY HAT AT HIS HIP AND WHIP IN HAND, "L'IL CLEM," *BELOW,* IS ABOUT THE SWEETEST COWPOKE IMAGINABLE. THE TEXTURES OF CLEM'S HAIR, LEATHER CHAPS, AND GATHERED NECKERCHIEF ARE EXPERTLY EXPRESSED IN THE SIX-INCH ORNAMENT.

Through the Eyes of a Child

THE LIGHT FANTASTIC

HOW TO CREATE ELECTRIFYING EFFECTS

CHRISTOPHER'S belief that more can be wonderful is nowhere more evident than when it comes to Christmas tree lights. The more light, the more sparkle, the more magic. Plan on plenty of time for this time-consuming task and you will be well rewarded. Christopher allows a day just for applying lights before moving on to ornaments. He likes to use miniature lights, the larger C-7s, which are UL approved for indoor use, and novelties like candle lights and bubble lights. Each kind uses different wattage and must only be attached to the same kind of light. Wear gloves to protect your hands from sharp needles. Rubber gloves work better than regular work gloves, since they allow you to better feel what you are doing.

To begin stringing the lights, plug in the first set and run the cord along the trunk. Work your way out from the inside along a main branch, wrapping the string of lights around the limb and any strong offshoots, then back to the trunk again. Then move on to the next branch. Avoid smaller side branches—the lights are too heavy for them. If you are using two types of lights, simply repeat the process with the second set. Proceed up the tree, plugging one set of lights into another matching set. Do not attach more than six sets of lights end to end, as this could blow a fuse or trip your circuit breaker, or worse, start a fire. Instead, plug each set of attached strings into an extension cord concealed on the trunk of the tree. Better yet, use a power strip with about six outlets and a surge protector. Be sure to ask someone in your hardware store how many light sets can safely be attached to one extension cord or power strip.

If you have an artificial tree, you can string a set of thirty-five or fifty lights on each branch and plug them into an extension cord in the center. This way, branches can be stored year after year with the lights attached, a significant time-saver. For another time-saver, some garden shops sell artificial trees that come with preattached lights, in either colored or clear bulbs.

Purchase all your lights from one manufacturer to avoid incompatibilities. Christopher likes to use jewel-tone lights with a few clear bulbs as accents. He prefers twinkling lights that glow on and fade off, but finds clumps of harsh flashing lights "just plain tacky." He recommends using quality lights such as those from GKI (800-666-6614), which cost slightly more than the drugstore variety but will light up reliably year after year. Some GKI light sets have an easily replaced fuse that is conveniently located in the plug.

KID STUFF

THREE ORNAMENTS REVEAL THE CARE WITH WHICH ALL SIDES OF THE MOLDED FORMS ARE TREATED. "OLD WOMAN IN A SHOE," *BELOW,* OF NURSERY RHYME FAME, CAN'T KEEP TRACK OF HER EIGHT YOUNG ONES, FOUR ON EITHER SIDE. TWO ON THE SIDE NOT SHOWN TREAT THE BOOTLACE LIKE A JUNGLE GYM. EIGHT OF THE KIDS IN "FIELD TRIP" (FOUR DIFFERENT ONES PEER OUT THE WINDOWS ON EACH SIDE OF THE BUS), *ABOVE LEFT,* LOOK WELL BEHAVED, BUT SURE ENOUGH, THE NINTH RASCAL AT THE BACK WINDOW IS MAKING A FACE AT THE DRIVER BEHIND. EVEN WITH ELECTRONIC GADGETS, KIDS WILL NEVER TIRE OF BLOCKS, BEARS, AND BALLS, ALL CAPTURED IN THE FULLY THREE-DIMENSIONAL "THE BEAR B C'S," *ABOVE RIGHT.*

Through the Eyes of a Child

SWEET DREAMS

"SUGAR SHACK EXTRAVAGANZA," *RIGHT*, LOOKS GOOD ENOUGH TO EAT, WITH ITS COOKIE ROOF AND GINGERBREAD SIDES STUDDED WITH GUMDROPS AND OTHER SWEETS. THE INTRICATELY DETAILED NINE-INCH ORNAMENT IS PART OF A LIMITED EDITION OF 5,000 PIECES. IN A VISUAL PUN, THE WHITE GLITTER REPRESENTS SUGAR, AS WELL AS SNOW. PERHAPS "GOLDILOCKS," *BELOW*, IS DREAMING OF JUST SUCH A GIN-GERBREAD HOUSE AS THE THREE BEARS AWAIT HER AWAKENING. THE OTHER SIDE OF THE ORNA-MENT DEPICTS THE RUSTIC EXTE-RIOR OF THE BEARS' COTTAGE.

Christopher Radko's Ornaments

While it is perhaps politically incorrect today, most children grow up watching endless reruns of cowboy movies on television and playing cowboys and Indians, and Christopher was no exception. His fascination with these uniquely American figures is revealed in numerous figural ornaments. "Will," a small boy dressed in chaps and bandanna and holding a lasso, is a perennial favorite that has been joined by his companions "Roundup," "Cow Poke," "Lean and Lanky," and "L'il Clem." Dressed to kill, "Quick Draw" mixes metaphors: He is a pig as well as a sheriff! "Dolly" and "Annie" acknowledge that girls love to get into the act as well. The depiction of American Indians in ornaments like "Rain Dance," "White Dove," "Sitting Bull," and "Wild Eagle" reflects Christopher's ongoing fascination with the world's numerous cultures.

Equally American is our fascination with baseball. Sports fans will cheer baby "Little League" and his big brother, "Little Slugger." Fans may not get to first base with the miniature bat called "Batter Up," but they certainly will cheer as they hang it on their tree. Lest they feel left out, football, soccer, and basketball buffs can choose beautifully detailed ornament "balls" from their favorite sport.

Profits from the tiny soccer ball ornament called "Matthew's Game" support the Matthew Berry Memorial Soccer Fund in Dallas, Texas. Santa Claus puts in a guest appearance as "Christmas Quarterback," and a winged "Angel Puck" gets some heavenly help as he zooms in for a goal.

Christmas was in Christopher's blood from an early age. "I was definitely the one in the family who was the most attached to the Christmas spirit and to Christmas decorating," he says. "It's just something that was always inside of me. I wouldn't just keep Christmas in the living room. I wanted Christmas in the den, the bedrooms, the kitchen, everywhere. And everywhere there was a little vignette with Santa holding a candle or a little wreath or a small village of cardboard houses, the kind you put lights in. I loved decorating all through the house." And his room was the place to start. Of the shiny aluminum tree (the kind that was very popular in the sixties) that sat in his bedroom, Christopher recalls, "I thought it was pretty cool at the time. I got some of the cast-off ornaments that were not considered pretty enough to put on the main tree."

But the main attraction was always the huge tree in the living room. Christo-

FAIRY TALES

DRESSED FOR THE BALL, CINDERELLA ALIGHTS FROM HER PUMPKIN COACH IN "ENCHANTED EVENING," *ABOVE*. THE ORNAMENT IS AN EXCLUSIVE STARLIGHT FAMILY MEMBERS OFFERING. THE TWO-SIDED "HANSEL & GRETEL," *LEFT*, HAS THE RUNAWAYS HIDING ON ONE SIDE OF THE EDIBLE HOUSE, WHILE ON THE OTHER SIDE THE WICKED WITCH AWAITS, BROOM IN HAND AND CAT AT HER FEET. CANDY CANE POSTS, CHOCOLATE LOGS, AND GINGERBREAD SHINGLES WOULD BE HARD TO RESIST. THE ORNAMENT CROWN FITS CLEVERLY ONTO THE CHIMNEY.

LICENSE TO PLAY

MEET AMERICA'S FAVORITE CHARACTERS

I<small>T</small> <small>ALL</small> started a mere four years ago when a representative of The Walt Disney Company approached Christopher to discuss the possibility of licensing ornaments depicting Mickey, Minnie, Goofy, and other classic Disney characters. For Christopher, who had regularly watched the Disney TV show on Sunday nights as a child, this was a match made in heaven. Now the world's most familiar cartoon characters have come to glittering life as ornaments that will delight and fascinate children—and children at heart—for generations to come. "They are characters that I grew up with in the early sixties," says Christopher. "They were a very real part of my childhood." Today, Christopher Radko has well over a dozen licensing arrangements with companies as diverse as Universal City Studios, Jim Henson Productions, Barbie-Mattel, Star Wars-Lucasfilms, North American Bear Company, and Harley-Davidson.

"My ornaments have always offered a chance for us to access an old-fashioned Christmas," Christopher explains. "Other subjects, such as Native American

themes, Art Deco, Egyptian, and to some degree the celestial designs of spaceships and martians, have been a departure from a traditional Victorian or turn-of-the-century Christmas. The licensed ornaments—representing pop culture of the fifties and sixties and even the early seventies—are in a sense yet another departure. And that's something fun to bring to your Christmas celebration." Whether they are traditional or contemporary in inspiration, Radko ornaments share one connection: They are about childhood, playfulness, nostalgia, and—a key word—fun.

And fun indeed are the glass figures of classic childhood literature as reincarnated in animated Disney films: "The Little Mermaid," "Peter Pan," and "Snow White," plus the Seven Dwarfs. Equally integral to an American childhood are the Muppets. From Kermit to Miss Piggy to Fozzie and Gonzo, the gang's all here. The fantastical creatures of the Wubbulous World of Dr. Seuss, including the Grinch, the Cat in the Hat, Horton, and Whozits, resonate for every child, every former child, and every parent. Not to be left out are the wacky Rocky and Bullwinkle and mischievous

Alvin and the Chipmunks. The dinosaurs from *The Lost World* have returned from extinction to hang on your tree. For more thrills and chills, watch out for our favorite monsters: "Dracula," "Creature from the Black Lagoon," and the "Bride of Frankenstein," to name but a few. "Chewbacca," "C-3PO," and "Darth Vader" observe a truce from their Star Wars only to hang from a Christmas tree. Another icon of childhood, America's favorite board game, turns up in a series of Monopoly ornaments. Everyone played with Mr. Potato Head as a youngster, and now the master of disguise even dresses up as a toy soldier on an ornament. No girl can imagine childhood without Barbie, who was "born" in 1959 and went on to become the world's most popular and fashionable doll. Muffy Vanderbear, the beguiling and well-dressed teddy bear, is particularly endearing in "Portrait in Black and White."

One of the most unlikely licenses is Harley-Davidson, but the results are fabulous. What could be more American than "Harley Santa," *above*, complete with shades and overloaded with gifts? (Turn him around to see the emblem on his studded leather jacket, his ponytail, and his key chain.) And in lieu of a stocking to hang by the chimney with care, "Biker Boot" is chock full of goodies.

Movies and television have profoundly shaped American culture, and many of the licensed ornaments celebrate movies or individual actors. Film-industry legends celebrated with ornaments include Charlie Chaplin, Laurel and Hardy, Jimmy Stewart, and the silent film star Harold Lloyd. And Lucy, Ricky, Ethel, and Fred, stars of television's most enduring sitcom, are commemorated in the "I Love Lucy" series of ornaments. "Candy Maker," *below*, recalls the famous episode where Lucy and Ethel work on a conveyor belt at a candy factory. For Christopher and his creative team, the challenge in designing licensed ornaments is to render the character exactly as it exists, then come up with expressive and unusual ways to turn it into an ornament. "We can't change the characters themselves, but we can play with accessories, positions, or themes," explains Christopher. And so the Cat in the Hat pops out of a wreath, Mickey Mouse dons a Santa suit and poses debonairly by a chimney, *opposite*, in "Rooftop Mickey," and Kermit the Frog auditions for a role in the Nutcracker Suite.

With numerous new licensing arrangements in the works, it is certain that even more of the icons of childhood and of popular culture as a whole will re-emerge on our Christmas trees as treats for the kid in all of us.

pher has no doubt that the Radko family Christmas tree was the most wonderful tree in the neighborhood. Even today, as the creator of the world's most fantastical trees, his voice takes on a note of excitement as he recalls the family Christmas trees of his childhood. "My favorite thing was the scent," he remembers. "The tree was always big and very full. We had lots of colored lights—and lots of bubble lights. They are hypnotic—it's like looking at a fish tank." And always underneath was a Lionel train chugging around the tree.

As a youngster, Christopher would invite friends over to see the tree after school, sometimes giving each one a list of difficult-to-find ornaments. The first one to find them on the tree would get a prize. "It was a challenge, since many of the ornaments were tucked in between the branches," he explains. "I loved sharing Christmas. I wanted to share that joy with other kids. I think I felt the joy inside of me, but my friends were actually expressing it in an extroverted way. Maybe they were mirroring it back to me in a way I couldn't express even though I was feeling it."

His favorite ornament was a mouth-blown glass anchor. "I remember that as a little kid I was not allowed to hang it because it was very fragile," he muses. "It was like forbidden fruit. As a three- or four-year-old, I didn't know that an anchor was used to moor a boat. I just liked the shape." Later his father explained that an anchor holds a boat securely even when it is floating in the water. "Inasmuch as a little kid can think metaphorically, I saw the anchor as a symbol of security," says Christopher. "It is tough to do new things, but if you have an anchor inside, you can handle anything. No matter how crazy the world is, deep down I feel that I am connected to something solid and safe." Now among the free-blown ornaments in the Christopher Radko line are an anchor just like the favorite one on his family tree and "Santa Anchor," which blends a free-blown anchor and a molded Santa, bringing together two of his favorite icons.

Another symbol Christopher has been attracted to since childhood is the star in all its guises. "The star symbolizes the night sky," he explains. "As a child, when I lay under our tree, which was always placed in a bay window, on a star-filled night I would see the stars outside shining through the branches and reflecting in the ornaments. It was pretty magical." Today, his company name is Starad, combining his favorite symbol with the first three letters of his last name. "I don't know why, but I used to count the stars in the sky. I would play games with them: If I could count twenty stars, the answer to my question would be yes; if not, I was in trouble. Somehow, I saw in stars a

source of comfort and answers. "Stars have a connection with infinity, beauty, serenity, and mystery," he continues, "but the anchor tethers me to the Earth. My humanness needs something safe; my spirit resonates to the infinite vastness of a star-filled night over a wide-open ocean." No wonder that the specific star shape that Christopher chose for Starad's logo is a navigational star, which allows a pilot to safely steer his ship at night.

As a child of the space age, Christopher's fascination with the star-filled sky is undoubtedly part of his intrigue with airplanes and space travel. "Ever since H. G. Wells and Buck Rogers, we've dreamed of setting foot among the stars," Christopher says. "Man's moon landing in 1969 made the connection between Earth and the heavens more than just a wish; it had become a reality." The significance of the moon landing opened new worlds of opportunity to Christopher's generation, and its implications were not lost on him. His first small collection of 1986 includes such ornaments as "Snow Comet," "Saturn," and the graphic black-and-white set of four

Through the Eyes of a Child

THREE-
RING SHOW

"MY FAVORITE CHIMP," *RIGHT*, WEARS A RUFFLED COLLAR AS HE WAITS FOR HIS CUE. "GERARD" THE GIRAFFE, *FAR RIGHT*, SHOWS OFF HIS BEAUTIFULLY MODU-LATED NECK AND LIMBS. "PONY EXPRESS," *BELOW*, GETS IN THE ACT BY SHOWING HOW HE CAN BALANCE ON HIS HAUNCHES.

PERFECT BALANCE

LIKE ALL CHILDREN, CHRISTOPHER WAS INTRIGUED BY ELEPHANTS AND OFTEN USES THEM IN HIS ORNAMENTS; "BALANCING BETTY," *CENTER LEFT*, IS A CHARMINGLY AWKWARD BABE, AND "ELEPHANTS ON PARADE," *LEFT*, DEPICTS THREE PINK PACHYDERMS. IN "BALANCING ACT," *FAR LEFT*, A CIRCUS SEAL BALANCES A BALL ON HER NOSE. EIGHT-INCH-TALL "JEST DANCE," *BELOW*, EXQUISITELY EXPRESSES THE HARLEQUIN'S JOY IN PERFORMING.

SPORTS
FANS

*Christopher
Radko's
Ornaments*

spheres called "Astral." A flurry of weather and hot-air balloons followed in later collections and before long, UFOs, and aliens were appearing as "Friendly Visitor," "Moon Martian," and "U-Boat," among others. Compared to them, the airplanes, zeppelins, helicopters, and spaceships that are recurrent motifs are downright down-to-earth.

Both Polish and French Christmas traditions were part of the seasonal celebrations in the Radko household. Young Christopher would come home from school in early December, turn on the tree lights, and put Christmas records on the stereo. "I remember playing French Christmas carols that my mother had bought at a store near Rockefeller Center," he recalls. "It was very different from American music, and I liked it a lot." There were also many albums of Polish Christmas carols. "They are distinct from German carols and English carols," he says. "But also beautiful. Some of them are like lullabies. Very sweet, very soft."

Christopher's taste in music was diverse. The family had collected dozens, perhaps a couple hundred, Christmas albums. "As a kid I was always buying the latest Christmas albums," he remembers. "I still have all those albums, as well as a million Christmas CDs!"

Christopher's love of music shows up in his ornaments. "Frosty" depicts the lovable snowman of song with the same name; "Lullaby" a babe in his bunting lulled to sleep by his mother's gentle song; "It's a Small World" a tiny clip-on globe. Christmas carols are celebrated in "Silent Night" and "Glory on High"; *Fantasia* is memorialized in a stunning reflector. Like many children, Christopher attended a performance of the Nutcracker Suite, and the limited edition ornaments of "Punchinello," "Mouse King," "Nutcracker Prince," "Sugar Plum Fairy," and friends recreate that magic.

Although he makes his living as a designer, Christopher does not recall having been a particularly artistic child. "At the time I didn't consciously realize how much joy creative efforts could bring," he says. "My mother always wanted to be an artist, but she chose medicine because it was safe, it was a sure job. My parents never said there was anything wrong with sculpting or painting, or drawing or being creative, but they never really put it out as a means for realizing yourself. Instead, hard work was the ticket. Being disciplined, being dependable, being reliable, getting really good grades, that was how you measured your success."

Christopher particularly liked ceramics. "It was always my favorite class," he remembers. "The only frustration I had in ceramics class was that the glazes never came out right. The reds would bake away when they were fired. Or the details I did would disappear. The colors weren't as bright as I wanted them to be." Today, the careful attention to detail and the wonderful rich colors are two hallmarks of a Christopher Radko ornament.

Another hallmark is quality. Christopher's ornaments are made of tempered glass (known in the United States by the trademark Pyrex, for example), which resists breakage and can tolerate changes in temperature, instead of scrap glass as ornaments had been traditionally. Ornament interiors are lined with real silver, not some cheaper and less beautiful substitute. Master molds are made of metal, which holds details longer than the ceramic molds often used in the past.

"When I was growing up I remember how the image on the toy box was always nicer than what was inside. The picture might make it look like a detailed house or a fancy truck with plenty of three-dimensional details, but when I took the toy out I found the details were only stenciled on. And of course the box would never show the rough edges on tin toys. I remember metal toys being rather flimsy in the 1960s. A hinge might be so flimsy that it couldn't hold a heavy D battery. One year I got a Spirograph, but I was frustrated with how the short pins would never stay in the cardboard, and if you went too fast they became dislodged and your picture was ruined."

Those acute powers of observation serve Christopher well today, both in constantly finding inspiration around him and in establishing the highest production standards for his ornaments. But most important, his attention to detail has enabled these delightful ornaments to provide all who encounter them a glimpse back into the magic of childhood, when anything is possible and everything is wonderful.

"TOUCHDOWN," *BELOW,* AND "BASKETBALL," *LOWER LEFT,* DISPLAY SIMILAR REALISM. THE TEXTURE OF THE FORMER'S PIGSKIN AND ITS STITCHING ARE FAITHFULLY IMITATED; THE SURFACE OF THE LATTER IS DOTTED WITH GOLD LACQUER. "ANGEL PUCK," *LEFT,* ENTERS THE REALM OF FANTASY. GOLDEN SKATE BLADES MATCH THE ANGEL WINGS JUST VISIBLE OVER HIS SHOULDERS.

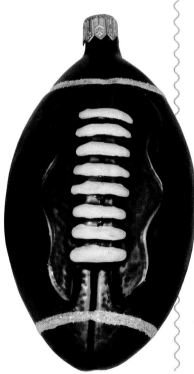

Through the Eyes of a Child

77

LET IT SNOW

KIDS LOVE MAKING SNOWMEN AND EVERYONE LOVES THESE CHILLY FOLKS. "CHUBBY CHEER," *ABOVE*, IS DRESSED FOR THE HOLI-DAYS AND CARRIES A BERIB-BONED GIFT. HIS SNOWBALL BODY IS COVERED WITH GLITTER-ING JEWEL-LIKE SNOWFLAKES; ANOTHER FLAKE HAS JUST LANDED ON HIS HAT. BUNDLED UP AGAINST THE COLD, "HEARTS FOUR YOU," *RIGHT*, ONE OF A SERIES OF STAR-SHAPED FIGURES, MAKES A CHARMINGLY UNCON-VENTIONAL SNOWPERSON.

COLD COMFORT

LIKE SNOWFLAKES, NO TWO RADKO SNOWMEN ARE EXACTLY ALIKE. "DRESSED TO CHILL," *NEAR LEFT,* A THREE-BALL MODEL, IS NATTY IN A VEST, SILK SCARF, AND TOP HAT. HIS COAL EYES, CARROT-STICK NOSE, AND BIRCH-BRANCH SWITCH ARE CLASSIC ACCOU-TREMENTS. PRETTY IN PINK, THE "LITTLEST SNOWMAN," *ABOVE LEFT,* STANDS A MERE 3 INCHES TALL, WHEREAS THE THREE OTHER ORNAMENTS ON THESE PAGES ARE ALL 6½ INCHES TALL.

HERE COMES
SANTA
CLAUS

SPECIAL DELIVERY

THE SINGLE MOST POPULAR ORNAMENT SUBJECT, SANTA APPEARS IN MYRIAD GUISES AND MODES OF TRANSPORTATION. IN "POLAR EXPRESS," *RIGHT*, HE HITCHES A RIDE ON A WINTERY WHITE BEAR, WHILE GLITTERING STARS LIGHT UP THE NIGHTTIME SKY. THE MOLD-BLOWN RELIEF DESIGN IS REPEATED ON THE OTHER SIDE. SANTA GIVES THE POLAR BEAR A BREAK AND MOUNTS A WHITE HORSE IN "MIDNIGHT RIDE" (PAGE 80), A FREE-BLOWN PAINTED GLOBE. HIS BASKET OF GOODIES HOLDS A DECORATED TREE, AN AMERICAN FLAG, AND, OF COURSE, CHRISTMAS TOYS.

HEN pressed to name his favorite ornaments, Christopher concedes that the Santas occupy a special place in his heart. And nowhere has his limitless imagination found more fertile territory than in his depictions of Mr. Claus. Each year his collection of ornaments totals close to one thousand, and about a hundred of these represent the figure that almost single-handedly exemplifies the holiday season. Like many beloved and

legendary figures, he goes by many names. Whether you call him Father Christmas, Père Noël, Kris Kringle, St. Nicholas, or Santa Claus—as he is usually known in the United States—Santa has come to personify the gift giver specifically and Christmas in its entirety.

To Christopher, Santa represents the spirit of generosity that is the best aspect of the holiday season. "Santa is all about love, about sharing and good cheer," he says, "and not just material things. He symbolizes the best part in each of us, the nurturing, benevolent person we want to be." Indeed, Christopher loves to dress up as Santa, complete with flowing white beard, fake potbelly, and wire-rim glasses, and bellow, "Ho, ho, ho!" when he signs ornaments for collectors.

Gift giving has always been an integral part of any celebration. Ancient northern European Celts exchanged gifts on New Year's Day. During the harvest festival of Saturnalia, Romans gave gifts of fruit, while the traditional gifts at Calends, their New Year, were branches of bay, olive, myrtle, holly, ivy, rosemary, or fir. Called *strenae,* these greens were considered symbols of life, health, and vigor. Later, *strenae* included anything sweet—fruit, cakes, nuts—or anything golden, which promises wealth, making gilded nuts and fruits popular.

Norse myths held that winter gifts came from their god Wodon. Berchta, an early Germanic goddess of the hearth, was another legendary gift giver. Usually portrayed as a hag and accompanied by elves and sprites, she rode through the land on winter nights at year's end, giving blessings and curses as appropriate to the recipient. Good children received gifts, bad ones

VARIATIONS ON A THEME

ABOVE, LEFT TO RIGHT: "HEARTFELT SANTA," BLOWN FROM TWO MOLDS, EXPRESSES CHRISTOPHER'S VIEW OF CHRISTMAS AS A SEASON OF LOVE AND CARING. WITH EVERY YEAR, HIS DESIGNS GET MORE DETAILED: IN "TOYS FOR ALL," AN OLD WORLD SANTA JOYFULLY BEARS HIS BURDEN OF TRUMPETS, CARS, SAILBOATS, TEDDY BEARS, AND MORE. "SAPPHIRE SANTA" DISPLAYS A DECORATED TREE AND A NONTRADITIONAL-COLORED COSTUME. BELOW, LEFT TO RIGHT: HANDSOMELY CLAD IN RED, WHITE, AND BLUE, "YANKEE DOODLE" IS A DISTINCTLY AMERICAN SANTA. "VINTAGE EMERALD SANTA" HAILS FROM RUSSIA WITH HIS LUXURIANT GREEN COAT TRIMMED WITH STRIPES OF GOLD GLITTER AND PAINTED PERSIAN LAMB TRIM. IN "JUBILATION," AN AFRICAN-AMERICAN SANTA WEARS AN EMBROIDERED AND ERMINE-TRIMMED CAPE, WITH A GIFT IN HAND AND A BELL HANGING BY HIS SIDE.

Here Comes Santa Claus

ROOM AT THE TOP

SANTA PROUDLY CROWNS A 12-INCH ITALIAN TREE TOPPER IN "SKY SANTA FINIAL," *BELOW*. FIRST THE GLOBE IS BLOWN, NEXT THE BASIC FIGURE; THEN THE GLASSBLOWER ANNEALS THE OUTSWEPT ARMS AND LITTLE FEET. AFTER SANTA GETS A PAINT JOB AND A SPRINKLING OF GLITTER, HIS WOOLLY BEARD IS GLUED ON. "SANTA IN SPACE," *RIGHT*, IS MADE IN POLAND. HIS SHIP IS FREE-BLOWN AND THEN INDENTED WITH REFLECTORS ON EITHER SIDE. DECORATION INCLUDES CRINKLY GOLD WIRE, ANGEL HAIR, AND A SPUN-GLASS TAIL.

lumps of coals or switches. People were supposed to leave out a feast for Berchta and her companions. Christians later renamed her Befana, and she became associated with the three gift-bearing Magi. When Christianity spread to northern Europe, the Church fathers felt that the gifts should come from a Christian instead of a pagan, so the job fell to St. Nicholas.

Unlike Wodon and Berchta, St. Nicholas was a human being. He was born in Lycia, a province in Asia Minor, in the third or fourth century A.D., supposedly on December 6. He was the patron saint of sailors, thieves, and of many other groups, including boys. (Later, in a more egalitarian spirit, he became the patron saint of both girls and boys.) Nicholas was known for his immense generosity. Born to wealth, he practiced anonymous deeds of charity. One of his legendary acts of goodness was to provide dowries for three impoverished sisters who otherwise would be doomed to lives of spinsterhood or, worse, prostitution. Before going to bed, they hung their stockings from the mantel to dry. During the night, Nicholas dropped bags of gold into their stockings, which they discovered when they awoke, finding themselves also suddenly quite marriageable. Paintings often depict St. Nick with his bag of gold, which has over time evolved into a sack of presents.

St. Nicholas's feast day on December 6 was traditionally celebrated by giving children small presents of gilt gingerbread or toys. In Europe it was the custom for a townsman to dress up, pretending to be St. Nicholas. On the eve of December 6, small children would leave out hay, straw, and carrots for St. Nick's horse. St. Nick in return would reward each of them with a present to be found in the morning. But St. Nick's generosity had a darker side. Nicholas was often accompanied by Klaubauf, or Black Peter, a furry, dark, horned creature with a long red tongue. This devilish monster was said to carry a black bag with which to kidnap bad children. He is often identified with the switches and the coal reserved for miscreants.

During the Reformation, emphasis on saints diminished, including St. Nicholas's role as a gift giver; instead, Christmas gifts were supposed to come from the Christ child, known as Christkindl in Germany. In the New World,

Christkindl translated into Chris Kringle, although by then the religious significance had been lost. In Dutch New Amsterdam, St. Nicholas re-emerged as a favorite figure called Sinterklaas. Instead of stockings, children would place their wooden clogs by the fireplace to catch gifts he tossed down the chimney. The earthly and the heavenly images had merged, with the earthly image becoming the dominant one.

The American press played a large role in popularizing Santa Claus. Tall, thin, and dressed as a bishop, a rather stern St. Nicholas was depicted by Washington Irving in 1809 in his *History of New*

CLEAR EVIDENCE

A GLASS SANTA PREPARES TO DESCEND A CHIMNEY IN "MIDNIGHT VISIT," *ABOVE.* ENCLOSED IN A CLEAR TEMPERED-GLASS BUBBLE, THE INTRICATE ORNAMENT SUGGESTS ONE OF THE SNOW GLOBES CHRISTOPHER ALSO CREATES. DELIGHTFUL DETAILS INCLUDE A BRISTLE TREE, A PIPECLEANER CANDY CANE, AND A COTTONY BALL ON ST. NICK'S STOCKING CAP. THE GLASS COMPONENTS ARE FREE-BLOWN, WITH SNOWFLAKES DABBED ON THE CLEAR GLASS BUBBLE AND RENDERED MORE PRECISELY ON THE BLUE-LACQUERED BASE.

THE BIRTH OF A MOLDED ORNAMENT

A MULTI-STEP PROCESS FOR EACH SHAPE

EVERY mold-blown glass ornament starts its life as a drawing, rendered to show all sides of the design. Next, working with Christopher, a master carver executes what is called a "figural" sculpted in clay or plaster, a process that often takes several passes to get it right. A Santa may look too squat, a bunny's ears too long, an angel's wings not as sharply defined as they should be.

When the figural is finally perfect, the mold maker's job begins. He makes a wax copy of the carving, which is then pressed into a snug container and buried in fireclay powder. A channel is cut in the top of the box and through the fireclay to reach the wax figure. When molten metal is poured into the hole, it instantly liquifies the wax, which seeps into the powdered clay. The space formerly occupied by the wax is replaced by metal, which cools in minutes, replicating the shape the wax figure once had. This new metal figure provides a durable record of the carved design. This master mold—or mother mold—then has its rough edges smoothed and is polished before negative molds are made from it. Using the "lost wax" process again, wax molds are taken from the metal casting and converted into metal molds.

Molds are made in two pieces with handles attached to facilitate use. Originally, molds used to shape ornaments were made of ceramic; however, after frequent use, this material lost much of its sharp detail, so later ornaments were not of the same quality as earlier ones. Instead of ceramic, all Radko ornaments are cast from metal molds, like those used for glass jewelry, where precise detail is essential to mimic the look of faceted jewels.

Each glass creation starts its life as a rod of clear tempered glass. The glassblower heats the rod to a high temperature in a gas flame, snipping off a small section that he blows quickly into an oval of glass. He then places the heated glass in a mold clamped to the forge and operated with a foot pedal. The two parts of the mold are pressed together, the glassblower gives a quick puff, and a glass Santa, teddy bear, or angel is born. The craftsman opens the form and places the ornament in the flame again to temper, or cure, it, making it stronger and more stable.

DAY SHIFT

ONE WOULD THINK SANTA WAS BUSY ENOUGH PREPARING FOR HIS NIGHT JOB, BUT HE HAS PLENTY OF OTHER INTERESTS, BOTH PROFESSIONAL AND EXTRACURRICULAR. OLD-FASHIONED "DR. SANTA," *ABOVE LEFT,* MAKES HOUSE CALLS—BUT ONLY ON DECEMBER 25. "MERRY MAILMAN," *BELOW LEFT,* LUGS A SACK SPILLING OUT MISSIVES INSTEAD OF THE USUAL GIFTS. AND IN HIS MOMENTS OF LEISURE, "JACK ST. NICHOLAS," *LEFT,* TEES OFF, COMPLETE WITH TWEED JACKET AND ARGYLE SOCKS.

REST
AND
RELAXATION

SANTA ENJOYS A FEW BREAKS IN
HIS KILLER SCHEDULE. *CLOCKWISE
FROM TOP LEFT:* OUTSIDE "SANTA'S
SHROOM," A SHOWROOM IN A
MUSHROOM, ST. NICK TAKES A
BREAK FROM CRAFTING AND
WRAPPING GIFTS. HOLDING A
DOVE OF PEACE AND A WREATH
OF HOLLY, A SYMBOL OF ETERNAL
LIFE, SANTA RINGS IN THE SEASON
IN THE BERIBBONED "NICK
O'BELL". HE CUDDLES UP WITH
HIS TRUSTY COMPANION IN "NICK
& RUDY"—NOTE THE REIN-
DEER'S HARNESS OF BELLS. A CAT
ON HIS LAP AND A MUG OF COF-
FEE IN HAND, AN EXHAUSTED
SANTA SOAKS HIS TIRED DOGS IN
"THE MORNING AFTER."

York from the Beginning of the World to the End of the Dutch Dynasty. Clement Clark Moore's poem *A Visit from St. Nicholas* (now known as *'Twas the Night Before Christmas*), first published in 1823, described Santa as "a right jolly old elf, . . . [with] a little round belly," a tiny sleigh, and eight reindeer. But it wasn't until 1863, when a Thomas Nast cartoon of Santa as a jolly, plump, bearded elf with a retinue of helpers was published in *Harper's Weekly,* that our present-day image of the jovial figure evolved. In 1931, paintings of Santa by Haddon Sundblom advertised Coca-Cola in *Look* and *Life* magazines and eliminated the elfishness, making Santa a grandfatherly giant over six feet tall. This Americanized version of Santa is now popular around the world.

To Christopher, the divergent ideas of a rather formal figure and a jolly one represent what he calls the European and the American sensibilities of Santa Claus. This divergence is apparent in his ornament designs for the two kinds of Santa. The European Santa is slim and wears a long robe trimmed in fur. He was the one most often depicted by the original glass-ornament makers: stern, dressed in old-style robes with his arms tucked in his sleeves or holding a pine tree. In contrast, the American Santa is usually plump, wears a short, fur-trimmed red jacket, and often is laden with gifts. "I see the jolly Santa," says Christopher, "as the idealized grandfather we all wish we had,

someone who holds you on his knees and tells you stories, someone who is generous with hugs." Unlike the stern Euro-Santa, this roly-poly figure would never carry a switch or threaten children with punishment.

However, when it comes to fashion, the European figure is leaps and bounds ahead of his American cousin. European-style Santa ornaments come in a dazzling array of magnificent robes, ranging from winter white to tuxedo black, princely purple, even aquamarine, recalling priestly robes worn on holy days. Their names are equally regal: "The Bishop," "Westminster Santa," "Romanov Santa." To this day, Santa continues to change his name, and literally change his colors. For example, under Communism, Santa Claus was persona non grata in the Soviet Union. Instead there was "Grandfather Frost," who resembled Santa but often wore a white or light blue coat. To celebrate the end of Communism, Christopher issued a Russian Santa in regal red.

Ornaments depict the jolly elf Santas in glorious variety, making ornaments in the workshop, poking out of a stocking, sitting on top of the world, emerging from the chimney, and saddling up a reindeer. The names of some of these figural ornaments reveal Christopher's sense of humor and love of wordplay. Witness "The Morning After" (a weary Santa soaking his feet); "Surf's Up" (Santa in a swimsuit on a surfboard); and "Riding

SEATED ON ONE TOADSTOOL AND SHIELDED BY ANOTHER, ONE OF SANTA'S ELVES TAKES A BREAK FROM HIS SHIFT IN THE TOY WORKSHOP. "ELFIN," *LEFT,* IS 5 INCHES TALL AND MADE BY POLISH CRAFTSMEN. ALTHOUGH MUSHROOM ORNAMENTS HAVE BEEN FREE-BLOWN FOR OVER A CENTURY, THIS MORE SOPHISTICATED ORNAMENT IS MOLD-BLOWN. IN EUROPE, MUSHROOMS ARE A TRADITIONAL SYMBOL OF GOOD FORTUNE. WITH HIS HEART-SHAPED HEAD AND GNOME-LIKE FACE, "GOTTA LOVE HIM," *BELOW,* LIVES UP TO HIS NAME. THIS ELF MAY NOT BE HANDSOME, BUT CHECK OUT THOSE FAB EYELASHES!

Here Comes Santa Claus

TO THE
MANNER
BORN

STANDING 9 INCHES TALL, THE
IMPOSING BUT CHARMING
"ROMANOV SANTA" IS GARBED IN
FLOWING CRIMSON GARMENTS.
THE SKIRT OF HIS ROBE IS PART
OF THE FREE-BLOWN GLASS
ORNAMENT PAINTED WITH GOLD
FILIGREE, BUT HIS MANTLE IS
CLOTH, BANDED IN EMBROI-
DERED RIBBON, FROM WHICH A
CROWN OF GOLD PEEKS OUT.
SANTA'S COSTUME IS FURTHER
ORNAMENTED WITH GOLD BRAID
AND HE HOLDS A STAR-TOPPED
STAFF AND A BRISTLE TREE. NOTE
THE TINY PAIR OF ICE SKATES
ATTACHED TO HIS WAIST.

SUGGESTING THE DOMES ON
RUSSIAN ORTHODOX CHURCHES,
"PEPPERMINT TWIST" FEATURES A
TRIO OF CAVORTING SANTAS.
SHOWN SLIGHTLY LARGER THAN
ITS 6½ INCH HEIGHT, THE
CAROUSEL IS FREE-BLOWN FROM
ONE PIECE OF GLASS BEFORE THE
SMALL FIGURES ARE ATTACHED.
THE GOOD-ENOUGH-TO-EAT
PEPPERMINT-CANDY EFFECT IS
ACHIEVED WITH ALTERNATING
STRIPES OF GLOSSY RED AND
SATIN WHITE LACQUER SEPA-
RATED BY LINES OF GLITTER.
THE BEARDS AND TASSLES ARE
MADE OF COTTON WOOL.

HOIST A CHEER

IN "HAPPY HANDFULL," *RIGHT*, AN
EXUBERANT AMERICAN-STYLE
SANTA GLORIES IN A MULTITUDE
OF GIFT-WRAPPED PRESENTS.
EACH PRESENT WEARS A DIFFER-
ENT RIBBON AND GIFT WRAP,
THEIR DESIGNS ACCENTED IN
GLITTER. HIS EUROPEAN COUSIN,
"BLUE BALMORAL SANTA," *BELOW*,
CARRIES A TREE AS WELL AS A TOY
SWORD AND SCABBARD, CLOWN
DOLLS, AND OTHER TREASURES.
CHRISTOPHER'S PASSION FOR
DETAIL EXTENDS TO THE PAINTED
FUR TRIM ON THE ELABORATELY
EMBROIDERED ROBE.

Bearback" (Santa on a polar bear).

Over the years a series of Santas has taken flight in a helicopter, a rocket, and a supersonic jet. Sometimes Santa manages without jet propulsion, riding on a comet in "Star Shot" or balancing on a moon sliver in "Crescent Cringle." When his head isn't in the clouds, Santa is equally at home on a motor scooter, a bobsled, skis, or a sailboat. He is as apt to be found in the kitchen baking up a storm as he is in the workshop crafting toys.

Just in case he might get lonely, keeping Santa company are ornaments of Mrs. Claus, his elfin workers, and his faithful retainer, Rudy. Although European in origin the elves belong to the tradition of the jolly American Santa, good-naturedly helping the boss make presents.

Early German glass ornaments often depict Santa carrying a tiny Christmas tree, which is appropriate considering that the other universal symbol of Christmas, an evergreen tree decorated with glass ornaments, was born in Germany. "Nothing is more glorious than a sparkling tree," says Christopher. To him, the Christmas tree is not just a Christian symbol. "It is a custom handed down through the ages, tran-

scending regional customs and faiths," he explains. "Both a wondrous sight for children and a passport to their own youth for adults."

The Christmas tree as we know it today evolved from a complicated tapestry of customs. Rooted in the earth, but with its spire pointing to the heavens, the evergreen has always inspired fellowship, hope, and renewed life. Early Celts worshiped trees as gods and regarded them as symbols of fruitfulness, even in the barrenness of winter. Druids in the British Isles believed that the spirits that lived in the forests entered the evergreen boughs when winter fell. Cuttings of greens were used in religious rites to ensure that vegetation would once again return to the barren earth, to brighten homes, and to guard against evil spirits. Connection between the Yule tree and the Christmas tree is more tenuous. Always an evergreen, the Yule tree was planted beside the entrance door or in a forecourt. Later on the Yule tree was brought indoors and kept in a box or tub, where it was watered and nurtured, as a reminder that Nature was not dead, but merely sleeping. Yule trees were never decorated.

Here Comes Santa Claus

DECORATING
WITH ORNAMENTS

HOW TO MAKE YOUR WHOLE HOUSE SPARKLE

 HY SHOULD WE confine Christmas ornaments only to the tree when their sparkle and beauty can enliven every room of the house?

❊ Place several of your favorite ornaments and a few solid-color globes in a glass or crystal bowl, arranging them so the caps are hidden. Or tie a small bow to each spring pin at the top. You can even hide a few broken ornaments at the bottom.

❊ Fill a grapevine cornucopia (you can spray it with gold paint if desired) with greenery, moss, or dried baby's breath. Place it on a table and arrange fruit and vegetable ornaments to spill out, perhaps mixing them with the real thing for a fuller look. Poke in a few heads of dried wheat or colorful berries for added texture.

❊ Tie a bow around a pillar candle or candlestick and attach a small ornament.

❊ At a dinner party, use an ornament or two at each place setting, tied to a napkin holder as a favor.

❊ Accent a drapery tieback with a single ornament or several in a theme. Perch clip-on birds and other clip-ons at the corners of your window treatments.

❊ Instead of mistletoe, hang a romantic ornament, perhaps a heart, at the head of your bed; or secure four ornaments to the corners of a four-poster.

❊ Hang ornaments from nylon filament or ribbon at the window. Be careful to avoid places that get a lot of sun, which could fade paint colors.

❊ Top a gift with an ornament, tied on with a beautiful bow. Tiny nuts and acorns work well, or go all out with one of the more elaborate figurals.

❊ Display themed ornaments, such as Santas or shells or stars, en masse on a mantel or curio cabinet, or on a metal ornament tree or feather tree.

❊ Suspend wreaths from wired French ribbon inside windows, then deck them with glass ornaments.

❊ Tie small wreaths or sprays on the back of dining chairs with a festive bow for a dinner party.

❊ Weave a real evergreen or artificial garland around your banister, then attach ornaments and lights.

❊ Hang a mistletoe kissing ball from a chandelier or door frame. Attach a few small berry or heart ornaments to a small foam ball, tuck in mistletoe and dried flowers, and finish it off with a ribbon or decorative cord.

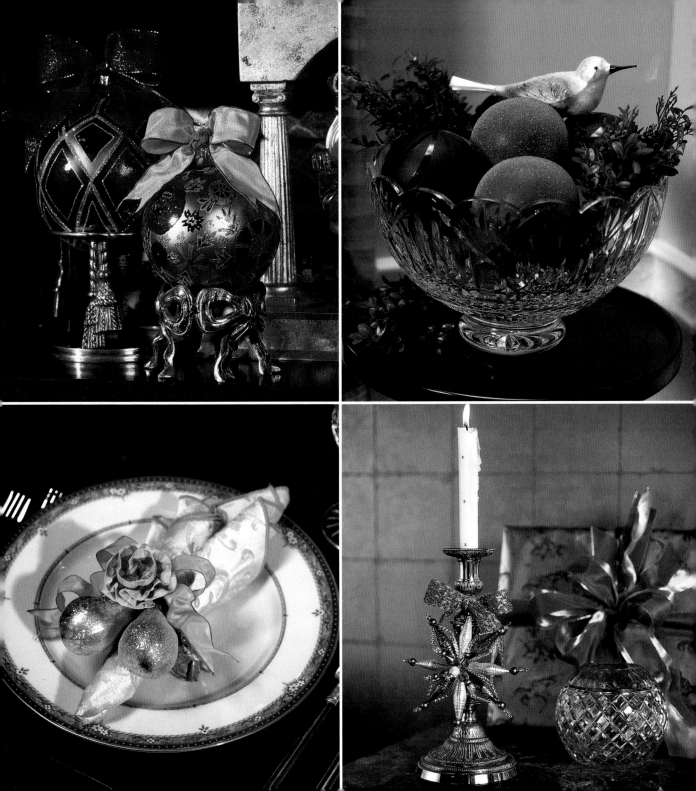

HIT THE ROAD

JOLLY ST. NICK SETS OUT IN "ROYAL ROADSTER," *BELOW*, TO DELIVER STILL MORE GIFTS. HIS ROYAL BLUE VEHICLE SPORTS CURVACEOUS GOLD HAND-TOOLING AND FANCY WHEEL RIMS ADORNED WITH HOLLY LEAVES AND BERRIES. THE FULL-TO-CAPACITY LOAD INCLUDES CLOWN DOLLS, STUFFED TOY MONKEYS, A DOLLHOUSE, A BALL, AND MORE DELIGHTS FOR GOOD LITTLE CHILDREN. A SINGLE HEADLIGHT WILL GUIDE SANTA THROUGHOUT THE NIGHT.

As they did with many pagan customs, the Christian church absorbed the tree into its iconography. The legend of St. Boniface, also known as St. Wynfrid, the English monk who organized the Christian church in Germany, tells how he came upon a group of pagan worshipers led by the Alemannic chieftain Gundhar. To celebrate the winter solstice, they were gathered around a large oak tree about to sacrifice Gundhar's oldest son to the god Thor. (The oak was sacred to Thor.) Boniface flattened the oak with one mighty blow of his sword, and in its place a tiny fir tree sprang up, thus demonstrating that Thor was powerless. Boniface told the pagans that the fir was the tree of life and represented the Christ child. In one fell swoop, he saved the life of Gundhar's son and furthered his conversion efforts. Legend has it that the little tree was taken to Gundhar's great hall and set up as the first Christmas tree.

There is another contender for the title of first Christmas tree. A tale tells of three trees, an olive, a date, and a pine tree, that stood near the manger in Bethlehem when the Christ child was born. The olive tree gave the infant a fruit, and the date did the same. The poor pine tree had nothing to give, so the stars came down to rest on the pine's boughs, turning the humble tree into the first Christmas tree.

During the fourteenth and fifteenth centuries, the pine tree also played a role in the miracle plays used to teach commoners about Christianity. In the story of Adam and Eve, which was often performed on Christmas Eve, a necessary prop was an apple tree. In winter a tree bearing fruit would not be available, so an evergreen adorned with apples and later communion wafers as well would stand in. The apples symbolized man's fall from grace, the communion wafers his opportunity for salvation. These trees of life, as they were called, are thought to be the origin of the traditional Christmas colors of red, white, and green.

The custom of the Christmas pyramid also began in northern Germany. A wooden form whose shape suggested a stylized evergreen tree would be wrapped with evergreen boughs, then hung with baubles, sweets, and gifts. A star and candle at top served as a symbolic welcome to the Christ child.

These diverse customs came together in Alsace late in the sixteenth century with the custom of decorating a Christmas tree with ornaments and candles. The origins of the tree as we know it today were now firmly planted. Along with Santa Claus, the two icons are inextricably entwined in our celebrations.

*Here
Comes
Santa Claus*

PILE IT ON

"SANTA BONANZA," *NEAR RIGHT,*
EXEMPLIFIES CHRISTOPHER'S PHI-
LOSOPHY THAT MORE IS BETTER.
PILED KNEES TO SHOULDERS, THE
JOLLY SANTAS ARE PART OF A
SERIES OF THREESOMES. EACH
ONE WEARS A SLIGHTLY DIFFER-
ENT COSTUME. "ROOFTOPS OF
LONDON," *ABOVE RIGHT*, IS A VARI-
ATION ON ANOTHER POPULAR
THEME: SANTA ABOUT TO
DESCEND A CHIMNEY. HE HOLDS
A TEDDY BEAR IN HIS HANDS,
AND IN HIS BASKET IS A MINIA-
TURE CHRISTOPHER RADKO HAR-
LEQUIN ORNAMENT. "BEACH
COMBER" SANTA, *BELOW RIGHT*,
ON VACATION IN HAWAII, TAKES A
LONG DRAW FROM HIS FROSTY
DRINK. IN BATHING TRUNKS,
SHADES, AND SANDALS, HE'S
READY TO CHILL OUT.

THICK AND THIN

IS "SECRET SANTA," *ABOVE LEFT*, SHUSHING US BECAUSE HE DOESN'T WANT THE KIDS TO HEAR HE'S ARRIVED? A STUFFED BUNNY TOY PEERS OVER HIS SACK, WONDERING WHO HIS NEW OWNER WILL BE. "CRANBERRY SLIM PICKIN'S" SANTA, *LEFT*, HAS OBVIOUSLY BEEN ON A CRASH DIET, BUT HE HAS A PEPPERMINT CANE READY FOR A SNACK ATTACK. THE 8½-INCH ORNAMENT IS GENEROUSLY TRIMMED WITH WHITE GLITTER TO ACCENT HIS SIMPLE RED ROBE. IN "UP ON THE HOUSETOP," *BELOW LEFT*, SANTA MAY BE HOPING THERE ARE COOKIES AND MILK AWAITING BELOW AS HE AND RUDOLPH LAND ON A TINY HOUSE, WITH A CHRISTMAS TREE AND PRESENTS AT THE READY.

Chapter Five

HOLIDAY BOUNTY

AMONG THE EARLIEST GLASS ORNAMENTS, FRUITS WERE RIFE WITH MEANING. THE PINEAPPLE, IN A REMARKABLY REALISTIC VERSION CALLED "HAWAII GOLD," *RIGHT*, HAS LONG BEEN A SYMBOL FOR HOSPITALITY. *OPPOSITE, CLOCKWISE FROM TOP LEFT:* "PASSION FRUIT" IS THE PULPY BERRY OF THE PASSIONFLOWER VINE, SO NAMED FOR THE FLOWER'S RESEMBLANCE TO CHRIST'S WOUNDS. "RUBY ORANGE" DEPICTS AN EXOTIC BLOOD ORANGE, A FEW SEEDS EXPOSED AND PRACTICALLY DRIPPING WITH JUICE. "SUGAR PLUM" LOOKS LUSCIOUS ENOUGH TO INDUCE VISIONS OF FAIRIES; IN ASIA, THE PLUM BLOSSOM IS A SYMBOL OF MAIDENHOOD BECAUSE IT APPEARS BEFORE THE LEAVES. "APPLE SLICE," DISPLAYING ITS CORE, RECALLS THE APPLE IN THE MOUTH OF THE SERPENT IN THE GARDEN OF EDEN.

AN YOU imagine a party without food and drink? Feasting is integral to any celebration, and Christmas is no exception. (In fact, all too often, overindulgence is the order of the day.) The sense of smell is said to be the most persistent of our five senses. The odors of certain foods, particularly those of dishes prepared just once a year, equally evoke powerful memories, transporting us to holidays past. "I remember just hanging out

and daydreaming by the Christmas tree, and Mom and Grandmother or one of my aunts were in the kitchen cooking," recalls Christopher. "I could smell the delicious aroma of food being prepared, and everything felt secure and wonderful." Such meaningful moments are suggested in "Kitty Cat Bake," a charming ornament depicting Santa stirring cake batter while a pair of felines rub languorously against the table legs.

Christmas holidays at the Radko home meant special dishes, and lots of them. Several weeks before the day itself, "things would start coming in like hints of Christmas—German strudels, gingerbread cookies, figs, sugar dates, and other sweets," says Christopher. At Christmas Eve supper, where visiting relatives would be guests, the meal combined French and Polish customs, but the Polish influence dominated. Traditionally, Poles serve no meat on

Christmas Eve. "You are supposed to have twelve separate dishes and none of them can have meat in them. So we would have a lot of grains, pasta, vegetables—including wild mushrooms (which are symbols of good luck in Poland)—and stewed fruits," recalls Christopher. French cuisine prevailed at dessert with the pièce de résistance: a *bûche de Noël,* a thin sponge cake spread with a cream filling and rolled up in the form of a log, then covered with chocolate icing decorated to symbolize a Yule log.

"Christmas Eve dinner involved a very drawn-out series of customs related to food," remembers Christopher. "For example, we would put straw underneath the tablecloth to symbolize the straw in the manger, out of view since Christ would not be born until the next day. We would always set an extra place at the

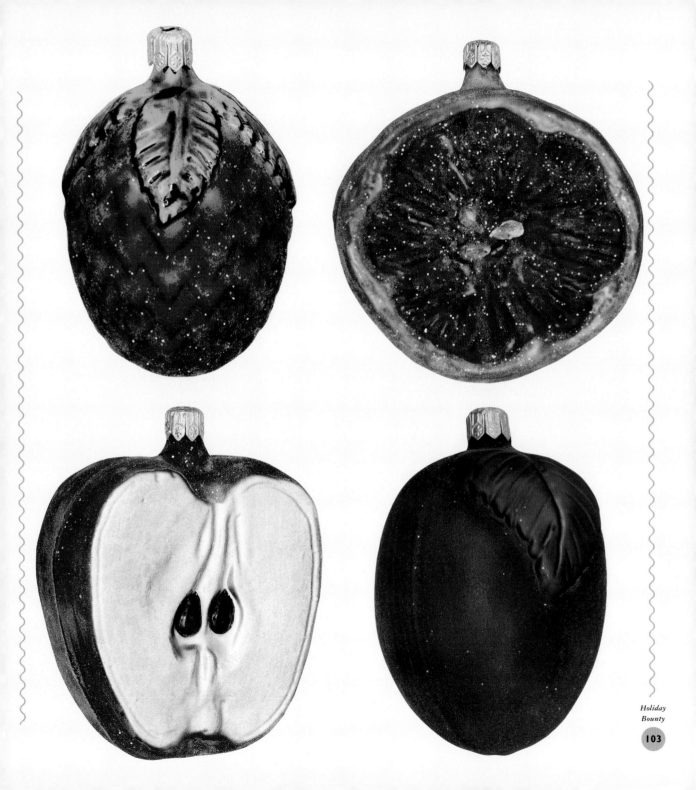

FOOD FOR THOUGHT

CORN IS A NEW WORLD CROP
AND WAS NOT POPULAR IN
GERMANY, WHERE IT WAS CON-
SIDERED FIT ONLY FOR SWINE.
AMERICANS KNOW BETTER, AND
"NATIVE BLEND," *RIGHT*, LOOKS AS
GOOD AS AN EAR OF JUST-PICKED
CORN. "FROSTY CARROT," *FAR
RIGHT*, LOGS IN AT A RESPECTABLE
7 INCHES. THE CARROT IS A TRA-
DITIONAL SYMBOL OF GOOD
LUCK IN THE KITCHEN.

table, symbolizing a wayfaring guest."

Since long before the birth of Christ, winter has traditionally been a time for harvest festivals that represent hope for rebirth in the new year. Feasting has always been an integral part of these celebrations, when people gathered around the groaning board to share good times and good food. The Greeks' harvest festival of Kronia honored Cronus, the patron of agriculture; the Roman celebration of Saturnalia was accompanied by two weeks of gluttony and abandon.

Compromise apparently was necessary to win converts to Christianity. Even as the new religion took hold, people were reluctant to give up old festivals. Christian leaders sagely incorporated many old customs into Christian rites and holy days. For example, although the actual date of Christ's birth is unknown, in 350 A.D. Pope Julius shrewdly selected the date of December 25 as the official Feast of the Nativity, borrowing the date of the *natalis solis invictus,* the birthday of the unconquered sun, on what was the winter solstice according to the Julian calendar. In 567 A.D., the Council of Tours declared the days between December 25 and January 6 to be the sacred season, and the twelve days of Christmas began. The actual word "Christmas" (*masse* is an Old English word for "festival" or "feast") was first used in England in 1038; the French name Noël (for Christ's birthday) appeared around the same time.

Christian leaders took a similar approach to adapting northern European festivals. Many of our Christmas rituals involve the very foods that marked pagan midwinter harvest festivities. During the Teutonic tribes' traditional twelve-day observance of the winter solstice, called Yule, many animals were slaughtered because the barren fields and scarce grain made it impossible to feed them. The boar was sacred to Frey, the Germanic god of peace and prosperity, so roast boar became a traditional dish that later turned up as a roast boar's head at Christmas dinner. Also handed down from the Teutons is the tradition of the wassail bowl, a potent mixture of hot ale sweetened with honey, spiced with nutmeg or ginger, and topped with a froth of roasted apples.

Perhaps the most enduring gift of the Teutons is the tradition of the Yule log, which they regarded as the symbolic mother of the sun god. A huge tree limb was burned for the twelve days of Yule, before being extinguished and the charred remains kept as protection against lightning and other evil forces for the year to come. On the twelfth night of Yule, the Teutons poured cider around trees as a way to drink to their good health and ensure

A CONTENDER FOR ONE OF THE BEST NAMES IN THE RADKO LINE, "HEARTY CHOKE," *LEFT,* IS ATTACHED UPRIGHT WITH AN ORNAMENT CLIP INSTEAD OF HANGING DOWN FROM A LOOP. ORNAMENTS DEPICTING PEAS IN A POD APPEARED IN GERMAN CATALOGS AS EARLY AS 1870. THE CHARMINGLY NAMED "PEAS ON EARTH," *BELOW,* REMAINS A PERENNIAL FAVORITE, THE PLUMP POD BURSTING WITH ITS TREASURE OF SWEET PEAS.

Holiday Bounty

TOP-NOTCH TOPIARIES

CULTIVATE A GARDEN OF MAGICAL FORMS

O NE OF the most charming uses of glass ornaments is as a component of topiaries, which come in myriad forms. Some are small, living plants coaxed into a particular shape—a ring of rosemary or a pyramid of ivy, for example. Others are plants that have been freeze-dried to preserve their beauty indefinitely. Still others are made of natural materials—bay leaves, lemons, or moss, perhaps—attached to a Styrofoam shape. Finally, there are topiaries with a shape that evokes a tree or bush, but composed of man-made materials. Each type of topiary lends itself to Christmas decoration.

Large topiaries can stand on their own, but smaller ones often benefit from being massed. Group several low ones on a dining table. Taller versions are at home on the mantel or sideboard. Try mixing sizes for even greater interest. Christopher Radko sells ready-made topiaries composed of ornaments, or you can make your own. Here are a few ideas to spark your imagination:

✳ Hang small glass ornaments and glass bead garlands on a matched pair of living or dried topiaries and place them on either side of the sideboard or at either end of the dining table. Decorate them the same or use glass fruits on one, vegetables on another. Feel free to add feathers, ribbons, or other decorations.

✳ Perch clip-on birds or other clip-ons of Santas, angels, or another theme on a living or dried topiary. Add some bows made from French wired ribbon.

✳ Hang a single special ornament tied with a bow from the top of a circular topiary of ivy or other greenery.

✳ Using a glue gun, cover conical Styrofoam forms with moss and silk or dried flowers. Then attach fruit or vegetable ornaments, using glue for permanency or florists' pins. Use a single type of fruit, such as strawberries or lemons, or use a free-form cornucopia of different fruits or vegetables. Another approach is to spiral on a limited number of different species, such as interspersing green apple slices with frosted strawberries and yellow pears.

✳ Using a similar treatment, attach gingerbread ornaments interspersed with peppermints and other hard candies for a sugar tree. Or use glass candies and plastic candy canes for permanence.

✳ Spiral a glass bead garland around a topiary form, attaching it to the Styrofoam every few inches with florist's wire.

✳ Be creative with containers: Consider gilded flowerpots, cachepots, metal urns, and pineneedle baskets.

✳ Use broken ornaments in topiaries by positioning the broken portion on the inside or covering it with a silk flower or ribbon.

HEALTH FOOD

CLOCKWISE FROM TOP:
CHRISTMAS-COLORED "SWEET
TOMATO" SEEMS ABOUT TO
BURST WITH FLAVOR;
"HOLIDAY PEAR" IS A LIFE-SIZE
4½ INCHES; "PEPPER'S FROST"
ALSO COMES IN PURPLE AND
RED VARIATIONS; "EGG LA
PLANTE" ASPIRES TO BE QUEEN
OF THE VEGGIES.

SWEET TOOTH

"GINGERBREAD TREE," *RIGHT*, GAR-
LANDED WITH ICING, AND "LET
THEM EAT CAKE" (*PAGE 100*), ARE
BUT A FEW OF THE DELECTABLE
GLASS CONFECTIONS TO HANG
ON YOUR TREE. "PRIZE PACKAGE,"
BELOW, IS A CAKE DECORATED
WITH GINGERBREAD MEN AND
FROSTING RIBBONS. THE TWO-
SIDED "SPICY FOLKS," *BELOW
RIGHT*, LOOK FRESH BAKED, BUT
THEY'LL NEVER GO STALE.

an abundant crop. As with many pagan customs, the Yule log was incorporated into the celebration of Christmas and would be kept alight for the feast's twelve days.

Around the world certain foods are inextricably linked to Christmas feasts, and rituals have sprung up around them. Spiced fruitcakes, candy canes, and roast goose immediately say Christmas. Christopher Radko ornaments such as "Cornucopia Frost," "Harvest Home," and the "Della Robbia" garland celebrate nature's bounty, and are equally appropriate as Thanksgiving decorations. No Christmas celebration would be complete without red-and-white-striped candy canes; likewise, no tree should be without at least a few "Mint Cane" glass ornaments and a "Penny Candy Garland" or "Candy Garland." Plum pudding started out as a

basic Celtic porridge of cereal, fruit, and meat before it took on festive airs in Victorian England. Everyone would take a turn stirring the mixture, making a wish as they did so. A five-penny piece was dropped into the mixture before it was steamed, and just before it was ready to serve, the pudding was doused with brandy and ignited as the grand finale of the feast. Whoever found the coin in his or her serving was said to have good luck for the year to come. Perhaps Jack Horner is looking for a coin in "Christmas Pie," a part free-blown, part molded ornament of a lad sitting on a purple plum eating his dessert with his fingers. A similar ritual takes place in France on *Fête des Rois,* the twelfth night of Christmas. In this case, the principal dish is a cake in which a bean has been hidden before baking. The cake is cut into as many portions as there are diners, and whoever finds the bean is crowned king or queen of Twelfth Night. He or she then picks a consort and, together, the "King and Queen of Misrule" command the other guests to perform ridiculous feats.

German Christmas specialties focus heavily on baked goods, many with wonderfully evocative tongue-twisting names: *Pfefferkuchen* (literally, pepper-cake or gingerbread), *Springerle* (hard cookies decorated as Christmas ornaments), *Lebkuchen, Nurnberger, Pfeffernusse,* and *Spritz;* plus decorated gingerbread houses like the one that figured so importantly in the tale of

Hansel and Gretel. Christopher recalls such delicacies in "Ginger Cracker," which is in the shape of a tin soldier, and in "Gingerbread Tree," "Spicy Folks," and "Ginger Hearts."

The French, renowned for their sophisticated palates, do not disappoint at Christmastime. The meal served after the family returns from midnight mass on Christmas Eve is known as *le réveillion,* meaning a late-night meal, and its menu varies by region, with local specialties taking pride of place. For example, in Alsace, roast goose reigns as the main course. Goose is of special import because legend has it that geese welcomed the Wise Men as they approached the manger where Jesus was

CREATING MAGIC WITH GARLANDS

HEIRLOOM JEWELRY FOR YOUR HOLIDAY DECOR

 OU CAN mix or match glass garlands just as you do ornaments. Use them alone, or interweave them with greenery and other ornaments, attaching them securely with florist's wire. Here are some other ideas:

✳ Arrange garlands on the dining table, snaking them among candlesticks and a centerpiece. You can tie two or three six-foot lengths together with ribbons, attaching a bow at each juncture.

✳ For a decorative fireplace, wire a garland onto the fire screen in a scallop pattern. For a working fireplace, hang the garland from the top of the mantel, keeping it away from direct heat.

✳ Swag one or more garlands over a mirror or a picture frame, or hang from door or window frames.

✳ Trace the graceful curves of drapery swags with a long garland, for what Christopher calls "six feet of instant Christmas!" Or use them as drapery tiebacks. Wire garlands to valances or pin them unobtrusively. Each garland has a hook at either end that can be attached to a cup hook for tiebacks.

✳ If your house has interesting architectural details, accent them with garlands. Spiral garlands around columns or swag them over an arch, using small nails to secure them.

✳ Hang a garland or two from a chandelier, scalloping them from arm to arm and securing with colorful ribbons.

✳ Weave garlands around the pine boughs or other evergreen swags decorating a staircase banister.

✳ Decorate a metal tabletop ornament tree exclusively with garlands, or mix with ornaments.

✳ Coil garlands in a glass bowl with sprigs of greenery, or mix ornaments, finials, and garlands.

✳ Put a candle in a footed bowl and spiral a garland around the inside of the bowl.

✳ Cover a foam topiary tree form with moss, then wrap a garland around it, securing with florist's wire. Meanwhile, gild or spray-paint a clay flowerpot gold. Glue the topiary to the decorative pot, add dried berries or silk flowers to fill in any empty spaces, and add a bow at the top.

OFF THE VINE

YOU CAN PRACTICALLY SMELL
THE INTOXICATING AROMA OF
RIPENESS IN "GRAPE BUZZ," *RIGHT*,
WHICH HAS ALREADY ATTRACTED
A HORD OF HORNETS. A FROST-
ING OF GLITTER SUGGESTS
THE SWEETNESS WITHIN.
A BUNCH OF GRAPES HAS
TRADITIONALLY SYMBOLIZED
FRIENDSHIP AND SHARING.

born. Bretons serve buckwheat cakes with sour cream, Burgundians turkey and chestnuts. In Provence, thirteen different desserts are served on Christmas Eve, symbolizing Christ and the twelve apostles. Sophisticated Parisians prefer oysters, foie gras, and *bûches de Noël*.

Although Britons may not have the gourmet pretensions of the French, they proudly cling to their traditional Christmas foods, with a single exception. Where once a roasted boar's head garlanded with greenery was the classic centerpiece of an English Christmas feast, today roast goose or a stuffed turkey is a more likely choice, served with sausages, potatoes, and brussels sprouts. Hot mulled wine or cider, Stilton cheese, nuts, and plum pudding round out the meal.

Sweets are important holiday foods, whether or not they are actually served at meals. Sugar cookies baked in shapes of stars, crowns, and shepherds' crooks were decorated and hung on trees before manufactured ornaments were available. Candy canes represent the bishop's crook of St. Nicholas, which itself is symbolic of crooks carried by shepherds, the first people to visit the Christ

child. In 1670, the choirmaster of Cologne Cathedral in Germany handed out sugar canes to young singers in the Nativity pageant, hoping the confections would keep the youngsters quiet during the long service. Many other foods have a symbolic, even sacrificial or sacramental origin. For example, a sprig of holly garnishing a plum pudding evokes the evergreen, symbol of everlasting life.

Long before they were decorated with glass ornaments, Christmas trees wore candied fruits, gilded nuts, bunches of grapes, even onions! More mundane potatoes and beets might be gilded to make them more beautiful. Paper garlands that traditionally adorned churches as a way to show thanks for a bountiful harvest appeared on trees, as did paper roses that symbolized the Madonna. Shaped pastries and marzipan replaced communion wafers, and the trees were known as "sugar trees" or "gift trees." Tropical fruits such as bananas and oranges, truly treats in the days before air freight, were later additions.

The first recorded Christmas tree in the New World dates to 1747 in Bethlehem, Pennsylvania, long before

Christopher Radko's Ornaments

Britain's Queen Victoria introduced the German custom to her subjects in England. The German settlers, known as the Pennsylvania Dutch, decorated their Christmas trees with fancy baked ornaments called *Krentslens.* Other ornaments were made of paper, cotton, and tinsel. These trees were typically small and placed on a tabletop, perhaps to keep them safe from the curious hands of children.

Ever ingenious, rural Americans used materials at hand to decorate their trees: garlands of popcorn—perhaps tinted red or green with vegetable dyes—and cranberries, corn-husk dolls, and other figures. Nuts might be gilded in gold or silver leaf. Fruits preserved in sugar, known as sweetmeats, provided a visual feast before becoming an actual one. By 1900, Americans were using room-height trees, rather than the tabletop size favored by Europeans.

By this time manufactured ornaments were fast replacing the homemade and edible versions. Not surprisingly, some of the earliest manufactured glass ornaments mimicked the myriad fruits and vegetables that once adorned early Christmas trees. The relatively common apple, plum, or banana could be free-blown; as molds came more into use, more complicated shapes like pineapples and sliced watermelons, pickles and ears of corn appeared. Baskets of fruit replicated the way flowers and fruit were traditionally carried to market. The German glassblowers delighted in depicting colorful and highly realistic pea pods, carrots, tomatoes, strawberries, and pumpkins. Most of these fruits and vegetables had symbolic meanings. Fruit in general represents the sweetness of Christ's salvation to man. The carrot is a harbinger of good luck in the kitchen, while the mushroom brings good luck in general. A cluster of grapes represents friendship and sharing, and a pineapple is an ancient symbol of hospitality.

Another symbol represents the benevolent sprites in Germany's wild pine forests: The pinecone (food to squirrels if not man) is widely believed to have been the first molded-glass tree ornament ever made. Decorating the tree with pinecones was thought to invoke the protection of the woodland fairies. Another early molded-glass ornament was the humble acorn, from which springs a mighty oak, symbolizing fertility and the cycle of rebirth.

PROMISE OF SUMMER

EVOKING THE LAZY DAYS OF SUMMER, "CHERRY JUBILEE," *LEFT,* AND "SUMMER SLICE," *BELOW,* PROMISE THE PLEASURES OF SWEET JUICE RUNNING DOWN YOUR FACE, MOUTH-WATERING PIES, AND PIT-SPITTING CONTESTS. "HAPPY HOLLANDAISE," 10 INCHES OF LIFELIKE ASPARAGUS, *OPPOSITE BELOW,* PUNS ON THE HOLIDAY GREETING.

Holiday Bounty

GOURMET
GIFTS

THE WOVEN BASKET IN
"CORNUCOPIA FROST," *ABOVE*,
OFFERS UP A BOUNTIFUL HARVEST
OF GARDEN GOODIES. FOUR
"COOKBOOK SANTAS" REPRESENT
A LIMITED EDITION OF 10,000
NUMBERED SETS. ONE HOLDS A
COOKBOOK, ANOTHER A ROAST
TURKEY; DESSERT IS A CHOCOLATE
CAKE, WITH TEA AND COOKIES
BEFORE BED. NOT TO BE OUT-
DONE, THREE "TEA TIME
CRACKERS" OFFER UP TEA, POL-
ISHED APPLES, AND GINGERBREAD
MEN. ALL THE SANTAS AND NUT-
CRACKERS DISPLAY THE SARTORIAL
DIVERSITY WE'VE COME TO EXPECT
IN CHRISTOPHER'S ORNAMENTS.
AT 7½ INCHES, "CANDY WRAP,"
ABOVE CENTER, COULD ALMOST
BE THE REAL THING.

SWEETER THAN WINE

"PETITE PIERRE," *ABOVE,* A SMALL VERSION OF A POPULAR EARLY CHRISTOPHER RADKO ORNAMENT INSPIRED BY THE LABEL ON A VINTAGE FRUIT CRATE, IS 3½ INCHES TALL. EACH PIT IS METICULOUSLY PAINTED, THEN LEAVES AND FRUIT ARE FROSTED WITH PERLINI. HIS PLAYFUL TOMATO AND STRAWBERRY COMPANIONS, *RIGHT,* FROM THE "TUTTI FRUTTI" CLAN, ARE FREE-BLOWN IN ITALY. THEIR CARTOONLIKE FACES MAKE THESE JOKERS EVEN MORE AMUSING.

Christopher has built upon this tradition of adorning the Christmas tree with ornaments that depict nature's blessings by offering realistic handmade fruits and vegetables. "My fruit and vegetable ornaments represent nature's gift of an abundant harvest to nourish and treat us," says Christopher. As with all his ornaments, he has taken these nature-themed ones into uncharted territory. Offerings include plums, pears, bananas, cherries, and pomegranates, just for starters. No child should have to be urged to eat his veggies ever again after feasting his eyes on Christopher's peas, peppers, cauliflowers, and eggplants.

Preserving a German tradition, bunches of grapes, plums, and other fruit ornaments often wear a frosting of Venetian dew, tiny glass beads that give the impression that the fruit has just emerged from the freezer. Others look like candied fruits, preserving an old Victorian tradition in which sugared fruits and nuts were considered true treats.

As always, the Radko wit is in full force when it comes to the naming process. "Panama Gold" is a perfect banana; "Banana Split" is a half-peeled version. "Vine Ripened" is a tomato worthy of the Burpee catalogue; "Hearty Choke" is a particularly clever play on words; and "Peas on Earth" puns as it celebrates the true spirit of the Christmas season.

In addition to the tour de force realism, Christopher has maintained another tradition of nineteenth- and early twentieth-century glassblowers. Complete with faces, and sometimes arms and legs, these vegetable- or fruit-shaped creatures have their roots in pre-Christian mythology. Today, Christopher's playful mold-blown "Goofy Fruits" and companion "Goofy Garden" vegetables and free-blown "Tutti Frutti" would bring a smile to even Scrooge's face.

Vegetables and fruit are good for you and Christopher's ornaments beautiful to observe, but we all need some treats in our actual and visual diets. Ornaments that depict cakes and other sweets are among his lushest. Feast your eyes on "Just Desserts" and "Let Them Eat Cake," and forgo the calories. Equally mouthwatering, "Nibble, Nibble" represents the house Hansel and Gretel came upon when they were lost in the woods. Good food deserves good drink, and the juice of the grape is celebrated in figures of wine and champagne bottles. All in all, these ornaments are a worthy toast to the culinary joys and flavors of the holiday season!

NUTTY AS A FRUITCAKE

"JAKE & ELROY," *BELOW*, ARE THE
COOLEST JAZZ DUO TO EVER
MAKE THE SCENE. WITH THEIR SUIT
JACKETS, PORKPIE HATS, AND
SHADES, THEY ARE REMINISCENT
OF A FAMOUS PAIR OF SOUL
BROTHERS. *ABOVE*, IN SOUTH-OF-
THE-BORDER SOMBREROS,
"BANANA BEAT," "STRAWBERRY
JAM," AND "PEAR FEVER" PREFER A
LATIN RHYTHM. THE HARMONICA,
TROMBONE, AND GUITARS ARE
ALL MADE OF PLASTIC.

Chapter Six

ALL
CREATURES
GREAT
AND SMALL

MADE IN ITALY, "PAPA BEAR
REFLECTOR," *BELOW,* INCORPO-
RATES THE POLISH REFLECTOR
TRADITION WITH A WHIMSICAL
ITALIAN DESIGN. "KIT'N BOOTS,"
RIGHT, A HAND-PAINTED, 7-INCH
TEARDROP, CAPTURES THE SASSI-
NESS OF PUSS IN BOOTS.

AN IS connected to the animal world both practically and spiritually. We rely on other species as beasts of burden and sources of food; certain animals have earned our friendship and love as pets. No wonder animals, both real and fantastic, have figured so prominently in the mythology of every culture. Witness the half-lion, half-human sphinx of ancient Egypt; Quetzalcoatl, the Aztec plumed serpent;

and the fire-breathing dragons in Chinese and other mythology. The Christian faith is equally rich in animal iconography. In the Victorian era, at least one snake ornament always hung on the Christmas tree lest anyone forget the serpent in the Garden of Eden. Christopher's brightly colored "Serpents of Paradise" acknowledge this tradition. Noah's ark, with its full complement of God's creatures, and the stable full of cattle and sheep where Christ was born, are equally filled with meaning.

With this powerful tradition, it is no surprise that animals figure as some of the most elaborately conceived and whimsical—and most popular—ornaments in the Christopher Radko line. "Animals do well," he says, "and cats and dogs do the best. People see animals as symbols for certain traits or powers they admire or wish to emulate," he adds. "The owl represents wisdom;

songbirds, a joyful spirit; and the lamb, purity or innocence. The fish as a symbol for Christ represents all the qualities of godliness." From the time Europeans first began making glass ornaments a century and a half ago, animals have figured prominently as subjects and have been among those most cherished.

In addition to the association of animals with daily life and the Bible, there was another reason why early German glassblowers may have chosen certain creatures as subjects. The artisans of the Thuringian mountains were also toy makers, and carved figures of animals that were then covered with chamois and fur may have served as models for ornaments of squirrels, bears, rabbits, hedgehogs, and other woodland denizens, some naturalistic, some delightfully whimsical. Mold-blown owls, penguins, pelicans, glittering peacocks, and songbirds were favorite

BEARS REPEATING

"ICE BEAR," *FAR LEFT*, IS A DESCEN-
DANT OF A BEAR WITH AN AQUA
BALL ISSUED IN 1993; BEARS WITH
BALLS IN SIX COLORS HAVE BEEN
OFFERED SINCE THEN. "SITTIN'
PRETTY," *LEFT*, IS PART OF A LONG
LINE OF MAJESTIC BIG CATS. HIS
TWO-TONE LEOPARD SPOTS ARE
BEAUTIFULLY PAINTED; HIS REALIS-
TICALLY RENDERED EYES SAY,
"DON'T MESS WITH ME."

※

RAINING CATS AND DOGS

"CHRISTMAS PUPPY LOVE," *FAR
LEFT*, PEEKING OUT OF A STOCK-
ING, WAS USED TO RAISE FUNDS
FOR CHARITIES THAT AID KIDS
WITH CANCER. HIS FRIEND
"FELINA," *LEFT*, FLAUNTS HER
JEWEL-STUDDED COLLAR AND
BATS HER FLIRTACIOUS EYE-
LASHES. SALES OF HER DAUGH-
TER, "FELINA'S HEART," BENEFITED
BREAST CANCER CHARITIES.

BETHLEHEM BOUND

subjects. In creations from beloved domestic animals to barnyard familiars to gaping alligators and omnidextrous octopi, early glassblowers indulged their imaginations and their technical skills.

Christopher's affinity with and respect for all creatures great and small began as a child. The Radko family always had pets, including dogs called Rex and Charlie, and Sylvester the cat.

Numerous ornaments, including "Rufus T. Dawg," "Puppy Love," and "Dizzy Dog" (playing a trumpet), are inspired by man's best friend.

In the past few years, cats have pulled ahead of dogs as Americans' favorite pet. The popularity of *Felis domesticus* is evident in the wonderful array of cat ornaments available. "Purrfect" depicts a pampered puss curled in her basket, a ball of yarn ever so delicately caught in a claw. "Shy Kitten" is the picture of innocence, while "Kitty Patch" perches on a pumpkin and "Black Cat" strikes an arched-back stance.

But cats and dogs are not the only favored animal shapes. Bunnies are so perennially popular that Christopher has created an ongoing mini-collection to which delightful additions are made annually. "Hop on Top," "Hopper B. Topper," and "Cotton Tales," to name but three rabbit ornaments, are equally at home as decorations for Easter as they are at Christmas. When it comes

BIRD HERD

"BLUE AMAZON'S" IRIDESCENT
FEATHERS ARE CAPTURED IN
LACQUER AND GOLD GLITTER,
ABOVE. "NIGHT WATCH," *ABOVE
RIGHT*, MADE FROM A VINTAGE
MOLD, LOOKS TYPICALLY
INSCRUTABLE. THE ATTENUATED
SHAPES OF WATER FOWL LEND
THEMSELVES WELL TO FREE-
BLOWN ORNAMENTS. "FLAMING
FLAMINGO," *RIGHT*, PERFECTLY
UNITES ANGLES AND CURVES.

to bears, Christopher's conviction that more is definitely better is in full force. "Tally Ho!" is dressed for a fox hunt; "Beary Sweet" is being cuddled in Mama Bear's arms; "Polar Coaster" totes an Eskimo passenger; "Ling Ling" commemorates a certain well-traveled Panda.

Inspired by religious icons, nursery rhymes, the circus, and his own love of nature, Christopher has built upon this solid foundation, elevating it to new heights with a veritable Noah's ark of creatures great and small. Each year's collection rains cats and dogs, fish and birds, bears and bunnies. Winsome mice snuggle in buntings, proud reindeer prance, lovebirds bill and coo, and languid lions lazily accept their due as kings of the beasts. Christopher's remarkable powers of observation, honed since childhood, are evident in the attention to furry, feathered, and finned detail. No wonder Christopher Radko ornaments are also sold in museums and zoos, as well as at Walt Disney World's Animal Kingdom.

Animals were an integral component of the Nativity and of Christmas legends and customs that followed. The three Magi are depicted as traveling to Jerusalem on the backs of donkeys or camels. Mary and Joseph arrived in Bethlehem on a donkey and, unable to find rooms at an inn, bedded down in a stable with cows, sheep, and goats. Cows are believed to have kept the Christ child warm with their breath. Legend has it that these barnyard companions, as well as wild animals in the woods, fell to their knees in adoration on the night of Christ's birth. In the German Alps it was long believed that animals could speak on Christmas day, but that no one ought to test this superstition. One curious person supposedly spied on the animals at this time and heard them foretelling his own death—and suffered the consequences.

St. Francis of Assisi, the patron saint of animals, is credited with being the first person to set up a crèche, complete with barnyard animals, to symbolize the setting where Christ was born. Other customs derived from the role of barnyard animals in the Nativity. In Poland peasants would dress up as sheep, oxen, and goats in remembrance of the animals in the stable, then march around singing carols. They would visit nobility and church dignitaries, begging for money and presents on Christmas day. In Germany, the tradition of St. Nicholas riding

WILD AND WOOLLY

through town on a donkey continues to this day.

The creatures associated with the Nativity appear in several of Christopher's most exquisite ornaments. In "Blessed Journey," the Madonna travels on the back of a mule accompanied by angels similarly mounted; astride camels in "From Orient Are," the three Magi follow the star to Bethlehem. Other animal ornaments are less specific in form, but embody equally powerful symbolism. "Rise 'n Shine" depicts a crowing rooster. In pre-Christian days, hens and roosters were long associated with the worship of the sun and were considered harbingers of the supernatural. Because the cock crows at dawn it is considered the guardian of light. Christians borrowed this symbolism, claiming that when Christ was born, the cock crowed *"Christus haues est"* in recognition of the arrival of the Light of the World. A rooster on a Christian tomb represented resurrection. The plain little hen, for her part, is a symbol of fertility and devoted motherhood.

The dove is an even more powerful Christian icon. Early Christians made it a symbol of the Holy Ghost, demonstrating how earthly love becomes divine. It is also a powerful symbol of peace and goodwill, in addition to communication, because of its role in carrying messages to loved ones. In biblical times, the turtledove returned to the Holy Land each year to breed and was there-

HANDLE WITH CARE
KEEPING YOUR TREASURES SAFE AND SOUND

 HRISTMAS ornaments, like any glass object, are fragile. But according to Christopher, his tempered-glass ornaments are as strong as a lightbulb. Like a bulb, if you drop an ornament on a rug, it probably will not break, and it has a fighting chance on a wood floor if not dropped from too great a height. The operative word is caution. Handle ornaments carefully and, if possible, remove them from their wrappings on a surface that has some padding. A tree skirt performs such a function in addition to hiding electrical cords and providing a finished look. A few overlapped lambskins are another option: They're soft and suggest newly fallen snow. Be sure the caps and hangers are securely attached (see "Tree-Trimming Tips," page 26).

It is natural for young children to be fascinated by ornaments, but if you have toddlers in the household, make sure rare or breakable ornaments are not within their reach. Or use an old-fashioned Christmas tree fence to keep the young and curious at bay. Speaking of curiosity, pets present an even greater challenge. One possibility is to spray the base of a tree with cat and dog repellant; again, hang breakable ornaments out of range of probing paws and wagging tails.

The paint or lacquer used on Christopher Radko ornaments is water based, so resist all impulses to clean them with water, glass cleaner, or other detergents, all of which could smear the finish. Instead, just whisk them with a feather duster, which attracts dust like a magnet. (A good mail-order source for an old-fashioned-looking feather duster made of ostrich feathers is Brookstone: 800-846-3000.) It is also a good idea to not hang ornaments in direct sunlight, which can cause delicate pigments to fade. Two weeks on a tree in front of a window is fine, because the winter sun is weaker.

When it comes to storage, gentle care will ensure that your glass treasures will be around for decades for you and your children to enjoy. Ornaments must be protected from extreme temperature changes and humidity—conditions often present in unheated, uninsulated areas like basements and attics. Such unstable environments can cause stress fractures over time. Instead, keep ornaments in a guest-room closet or some other temperature-controlled place.

A variety of containers and cushioning materials is suitable. Sturdy cardboard boxes, plastic containers with secure tops (such as those made by Rubbermaid), old-fashioned hatboxes, or systems specifically designed for ornaments, which offer compartmentalized storage, are all suitable choices. (Christopher Radko acid-free cardboard storage boxes offer forty-eight large adjustable compartments lined with fine jewelry cloth.) Keep in mind that plastic boxes are sturdier than cardboard ones, but a completely airtight environment may not be the best place to store antique or valuable ornaments.

Before being placed in a box, each ornament should be individually wrapped. Save the boxes that ornaments came in or use acid-free tissue paper (also available from Christopher Radko) or acid-free paper towels (the kind sold as microwavable). Never use old newspapers or even clean newsprint, as chemicals in the ink and the paper itself can damage the lacquer finishes on the ornaments. Christopher's preferred method is to wrap each ornament in tissue and place it in an ornament box or a large hatbox.

When you have wrapped each ornament, lay bubble wrap or loosely wadded tissue on the bottom of the tray or box. Then carefully place each ornament in a compartment. If your box has no dividers, use extra tissue paper to cushion the ornaments from each other. Place a packet of silica gel desiccant (available at craft stores), which will absorb moisture, in each tray.

Store metal ornaments that could damage glass separately. Also, ornaments made of dough or other natural products may attract insects or mice, so discard them or store them separately. Pack wreaths and other large decorations as you do ornaments, but store them separately, so there is no danger of their crushing smaller ornaments.

Finally, clearly label all of the storage boxes so you don't have to rummage through half a dozen boxes to find specific pieces, such as bunny, flower, and egg ornaments and garlands you will want to display at Eastertime.

MARINE SCENE

"MAXINE," *BELOW,* IS ALL LEGS, BUT "CHARLIE HORSE," *RIGHT,* HAS NONE. ONE OF A PAIR OF PIPES CALLED "DELPHINS," *BELOW RIGHT,* RECALLS THE DOLPHIN HEADS SPEWING WATER FROM ROMAN FOUNTAINS. *OPPOSITE, FROM TOP LEFT:* FREE AT LAST, "WEE WILLY" WHALE JOINS "DOLPHIN DANCE" IN JOYFUL LEAPS; "SHELL FINIAL" IS 13 INCHES OF IRIDESCENT GLASS, ITS SHAPE ECHOED BY ONE OF FOUR "SHIMMER SHELLS"; "DEEP SEA DELIGHT" IS PART OF A SCHOOL OF RAINBOW FISH.

fore regarded as a harbinger of spring and a symbol of rebirth. Like so many other icons, the symbolic connection predates Christianity. Egyptians associated the dove with the human soul, and dovecotes were built on tombs in Babylon as earthly homes for the soul of the departed. Turtledoves are said to mate for life, making them a symbol also of eternal devotion and constancy between man and woman. The universal appeal of this subject is evident in "Two Turtle Doves."

Storks are also considered harbingers of spring and thus rebirth. Ancient peoples thought that storks brought with them the spirits of the newborn, hence the myth fed to children in a more puritanical age that babies are delivered by storks. Christopher perpetuates this charming idea in "Stork Story," available in both blue and pink versions, of course.

Even today, throughout much of northern Europe, flocks of storks return after wintering in Africa. So eager are they to coax the giant birds into building nests on their property that farmers set up tall poles if they don't have trees or spare

chimneys. It is considered good luck to have a stork nest on your land, and once enticed the storks tend to return year after year.

The owl is another potent symbol, representing wisdom. Sighting an owl was regarded by the ancients as an omen that one would be receiving wisdom from a spiritual plane. But thanks to their graceful shapes and variety of colors, the most common subjects for ornithological ornaments are songbirds, symbols of joy and happiness. Originally, such songsters hung from a delicate glass hook, but soon the types of clips used to attach candles to the Christmas tree were appropriated, allowing the birds to perch in lifelike fashion on branches. Many of Christopher's bird ornaments, such as "Birds of a Feather" and "Autumn Birds," likewise sport spun-glass tails and are fitted with metal clips.

In northern Europe, charming holiday customs remember our four- and two-footed friends, paying tribute to the animals present at Christ's birth. Beasts of burden and cattle are given extra fodder at Christmastime. It is difficult for birds to find sufficient food during winter's snowy months, so a sheaf of wheat, harvested earlier

Christopher Radko's Ornaments

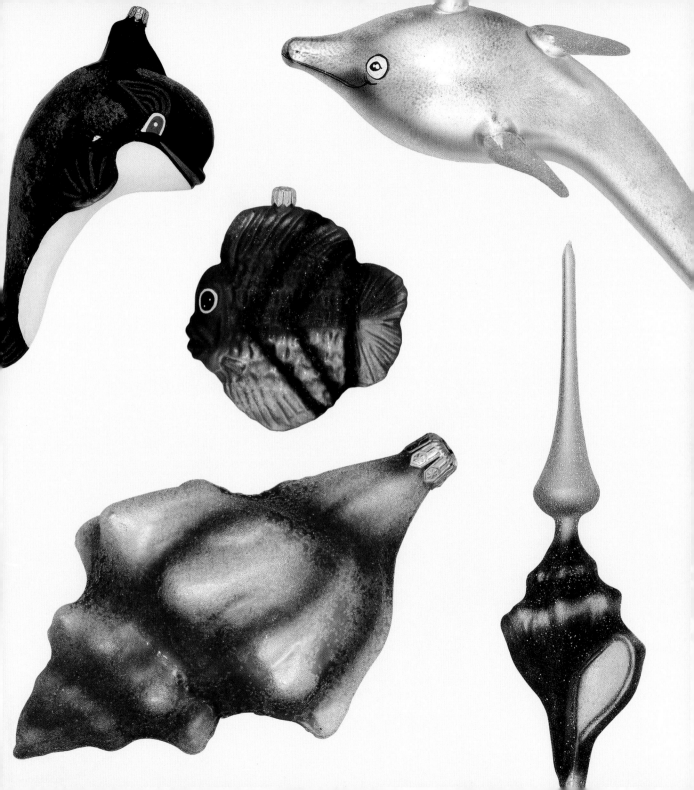

TO TOP IT ALL OFF

A FINIAL IS THE PERFECT FINISHING TOUCH

T REE toppers—also known as spikes, finials, and points—came on the scene in Germany in the late nineteenth century, and quickly appropriated the place of honor once reserved for an angel, a star, or a rosette. Finials typically were four to twelve inches in height, although some reached an impressive eighteen inches. They were often elaborately wrapped with crinkly wire or festooned with spun glass. Their creation requires the utmost skill, and the Polish artisans who make them turn out no more than thirty per day.

As always, Christopher has taken a traditional concept, then pulled out all the stops. Santas, angels, and other mold-blown figures perch on top of elaborate two- or three-ball free-blown spires, each made from a single piece of glass! With toppers this magnificent, you'll want to find other ways to use them. Some collectors place a wire hanger on the base of a topper and hang it like an icicle. Here are some other ideas:

✳ Create a tablescape with a group of candlesticks in silver, glass, or brass. Secure each one with a candle, and carefully slip a finial over it. Alternatively, use a half-inch-wide wooden dowel about twelve inches long. Secure it with florist's putty and cover the juncture with greenery, moss, or a ribbon.

✳ Securely attach dowels to a piece of one-inch board cut in a circle, square, or rectangle: slip on toppers; secure with clay; then cover the board with greenery. Add votives for enhanced sparkle.

✳ Insert a dowel into the top of a Styrofoam topiary form, then attach a topper.

✳ Place a block of florist's foam in a punch bowl or large vase with a wide opening, shaping the foam with a paring knife. Insert dowels in a splayed arrangement and slip on the toppers and secure with clay. Fill in the spaces with silk or dried flowers, draping greenery over the side to hide the foam. If you want to use fresh flowers, substitute Lucite rods, which will not wick water up to the finial, for the dowels.

✳ Hang toppers upside down in front of a large mirror with a silk ribbon entwined with some greenery.

OF PRINCES
AND KINGS

that year, is traditionally placed atop a tall pole on Christmas morning. Every gable, gate, and doorway is likewise decorated with sheaves of grain. The custom of decorating an outdoor Christmas tree for birds with suet balls, fruit, seeds, and wheat is a continuance of this tradition.

Fish represent rather complicated and even contradictory concepts. As denizens of the deep, they were thought by the ancients to represent fertility. But because they are cold-blooded, they were thought not to be governed by passion and therefore were considered sacrificial creatures appropriate for sacred meals. Their use as a symbol for Christ arose out the Greek word for fish, *ichthys,* which was used as an acronym for the Greek *Iesous Christos Theou Hyious Sotor* (Jesus Christ Son of God, Savior). The fish (specifically, the carp) became a secret sign that one Christian would use to communicate to another in the hostile environment of Greece in Christianity's early days. In Japan, the carp symbolizes endurance, courage, and strength. When a son is born, the Japanese hang a carp-shaped flag outside. Today, Christopher's brightly colored "Holy Mackerel," "Goldie," and "Parrot Fish" dangle from the tree rather than swim in their watery element, accompanied by dolphins, lobsters, starfish, sea horses, and other seafaring creatures.

Even insects are not excluded from Christmas fables or as inspiration for ornaments. An old English fable holds that bees hum Christmas hymns en masse during the holidays. A Czechoslovakian folktale tells of a spider living in the roof rafters of a house. It overhears the anguished sobs of a little girl crying herself to sleep because her family is so poor they cannot afford ornaments to decorate the Christmas tree, and she fears Santa Claus will pass her by. The kindly spider spends a whole night weaving a beautiful sterling silver web to decorate the bare tree. Made in the Czech Republic in traditional style by stringing tiny glass beads on wire, "Christmas Spider" depicts that benevolent arachnid.

Christopher's fancy was also spurred by animal characters in nursery rhymes and exotic creatures glimpsed in visits to the circus and the zoo. "Froggy Child," "Puss in Boots," and "Mother Goose" herself are all early animal figures. In 1993, when he started working with Italian glassblowers who specialize in elaborate freeblown figures, Christopher's menagerie expanded dramatically. "Gerard" the giraffe is all attenuated perfection, "Circus Seal" looks realistically wet and slithery, "My What Big Teeth" is a disturbingly well-fed wolf. Somewhere between fantasy and science, "Nellie," the sea serpent, and "Wintersaurus," a seasonally appropriate dinosaur, are safe from extinction.

Exotic species usually glimpsed only

IT TAKES TWO

IN THE TWO-SIDED "NOAH VACANCY," *LEFT AND PAGE 118,* THIRTEEN ANIMAL SPECIES ARE SAFELY ON BOARD, WHILE A PAIR OF PORPOISES LEAPS ABOVE THE ROILING WAVES BESIDE NOAH'S ARK. HIPPOS, MACAWS, GAZELLES, MOOSE, LIONS, AND RABBITS COHABIT PEACEFULLY, A LESSON FOR MANKIND. NOTE THE TINY OWLS PERCHED BESIDE THE ZEBRAS. SADLY, TYRANNOSAURUS "REX DANCE," *BELOW,* IS MISSING A PARTNER AND CAN'T BOARD THE BOAT. STILL, HE IS A REGAL CREATURE, HIS MAJESTIC BODY FREE-BLOWN, LACQUERED ROYAL PURPLE, AND DUSTED WITH GOLDEN PERLINI, BEFITTING THE KING OF THE DINOSAURS.

in books, on nature programs, or perhaps in a zoo, can also be tucked among the boughs of a Christmas tree. "Horse of a Different Color" is a handsome zebra; the big cats are well represented with the leopard "Sittin' Pretty" and "Frosty Tiger"; three penguins perform a balancing act in "Arctic Antics."

With his animal ornaments, as with all his creations, Christopher has populated a world of his own. These magical ornaments re-create a childhood more wonderful than any real experience could ever have been, where laughter is never muted by tears, where fun is never edged out by pain, where fantasy rules and beauty is eternal. This recalled and reimagined childhood is one of the greatest gifts that Christmas offers. However, it is but a first step. We have an opportunity to pass on that joy to our own children and all children. As breathtakingly beautiful as Christopher Radko's ornaments are, they merely open the door to possibility; it is up to us to reach our own unlimited potential. And spare no time. "Appreciate what you have," says Christopher. "Life is precious, and as fragile as a glass ornament."

All Creatures Great and Small

135

DIRECTORY

The Starlight Family of Collectors is the special club for those who love Christopher Radko's ornaments and holiday decor. Members receive an exclusive collector's ornament free of charge, one year's subscription to *Starlight* magazine, and a complete set of the latest Christopher Radko catalogs with annual membership.

To request more information or to join, call 1-800-71-RADKO. You may also write:

The Starlight Family
of Collectors
P.O. Box 775249
St. Louis, MO 63177-5249

For the latest news and information about Christopher Radko, visit the Web site: www.christopherradko.com

A bimonthly newsletter for glass ornament enthusiasts is of special interest to Christopher Radko collectors:

Holiday Times: A Newsletter About Christopher Radko Ornaments
Publishers: Steve Robba and Melody Link
484 Oak Tree Avenue
South Plainfield, NJ 07080
908-769-5711

STARLIGHT STORES

Starlight Stores are the premiere dealers for Christopher Radko's stunning collection of ornaments and home accents. All will be happy to take your phone orders and can ship nationwide.

CALIFORNIA
Corona Del Mar
Roger's Gardens
"The Original Starlight Store"
800-64-RADKO

San Francisco
Glass Pheasant
800-255-7179

CONNECTICUT
Wallingford
Vinny's Showplace
800-98-VINNY

FLORIDA
Vero Beach
Four Seasons Christmas Shoppe
888-HO-HO-HOS

MASSACHUSETTS
Boston
Christmas Dove
888-550-3683

West Boylston
Parker's Gifts & Collectibles
800-764-5151

MICHIGAN
Birmingham
Marley's
888-RADKO-88

MISSOURI
St. Louis
Botanicals On The Park
800-848-7674

NEBRASKA
Omaha
Borsheim's
800-642-4438

NEW HAMPSHIRE
Barrington
Christmas Dove
800-550-3683

NEW YORK
New York City
South Street Seaport
Christmas Dove
877-550-DOVE

NORTH CAROLINA
Wilmington
Abigail's
800-887-1616

OHIO
Worthington
Christmas Village
800-331-8543

OKLAHOMA
Oklahoma City
North Pole City
800-526-5829

Tulsa
Margo's Gift Shop
800-88-MARGO

OREGON
Lake Oswego
R. Blooms of Lake Oswego
888-30-RADKO

TEXAS
San Antonio
Christmas Gallery
877-85-RADKO

Tyler
The Christmas Store
800-241-4734

VIRGINIA
Alexandria
Christmas Attic
800-881-0084

Virginia Beach
Christmas Attic
800-881-0082

WASHINGTON
Puyallup
James Craig of Puyallup
888-41-RADKO

WISCONSIN
Oconomowoc
Pine Creek Collectibles
888-90-RADKO

RISING STAR STORES

Christopher Radko Rising Star Stores carry a large assortment of the ornaments and home accents from Christopher's collection. Their selection is slightly less extensive than at Starlight Stores, but, like those premiere dealers, Rising Star Stores will be happy to take your phone orders and can ship nationwide.

ALABAMA
Cullman
Bennett Home Supply
205-734-2961

ARIZONA
Scottsdale
European Christmas Market
602-233-2342

ARKANSAS
Little Rock
Crown Shop
800-353-8442

CALIFORNIA
Burbank
Sheridan Gardens
800-841-8846

Campbell
California Collectibles
888-377-9875

Chatsworth
Chatsworth Florist
800-248-1449

Escondido
Canterbury Gardens
800-214-WISH

Newbury Park
Angela's Florist
800-61-RADKO

Norwalk
Herman's Hallmark &
Collectibles
888-7-HALLMARK

Petaluma
Marisa's Fantasia
707-762-5804

San Diego
Creations & Confections at
Bazaar Del Mundo
888-296-4080

Thousand Oaks
Zender's Christmas
800-968-8366

Valencia
Cobblestone Cottage
800-599-9278

Woodland Hills
Deforest's Christmas Shop
800-80-RADKO

COLORADO
Parker
Kris Kringle's
303-840-1828

CONNECTICUT
Newtown
Lexington Gardens
203-426-3161

Oxford
Utopia Collectibles
888-886-7427

DELAWARE
Millsboro
Kitty's
302-934-9578

FLORIDA
Destin
Lindz's
850-837-8070

Fort Myers
Mole Hole
941-433-4700

Mount Dora
Karen's Gift Shoppe
888-527-3674

Orange Park
Annabelle's Ltd.
888-450-5544

Reddick
Wayside Antiques &
Christmas Center
800-228-2001

Tampa
Alvin Magnon Jewelers
888-823-3414

GEORGIA
Atlanta
Glass, Etc.
888-452-7382
The Mole Hole of Atlanta
800-252-MOLE

Dalton
Pickity Place
706-278-9368

Lilburn
Nature's Fifth Season
770-925-4600

Macon
One Step Further
800-699-4596

Rome
White Rabbit
706-235-2162

Savannah
Levy Jewelers
800-237-LEVY

Valdosta
Triphenger's
888-50-RADKO

ILLINOIS
Bloomington
Cydney's
800-899-4336

Champaign
JBJ's The Collector Shop
800-331-3229

Naperville
The Cranberry Moose
888-25-SANTA

Orland Park
Mitchell's Flowers &
Christmas
800-551-8475

INDIANA
Indianapolis
Graham's Crackers
800-442-5727

Newburgh
BJ's Flowers and Gifts
800-800-7381

St. John
Louise's Hallmark
800-889-6088

IOWA
Cedar Rapids
Artistic Accents
319-393-6588

KANSAS
Wichita
Plaid Giraffe
316-683-1364

KENTUCKY
Ashland
Traditional Creations
800-365-5069

Hazel
Miss Bradie's
800-455-9911

Lexington
Schwab's Collectible's
800-799-0006

LOUISIANA
Lafayette
Marshall's Home & Garden
Showplace
318-984-3230

New Orleans
Lindz's
504-581-2140

Shreveport
Lewis' Gifts
888-545-3497

MAINE
Ellsworth
MM Julz
207-667-2029

Portland
Country Noel
800-357-NOEL

MASSACHUSETTS
Nantucket
Nantucket Sleighride
888-NANTUKT

South Weymouth
Fosters'
800-439-3546

MICHIGAN
Franklin
Village Barn
248-851-7877

Hamtramck
Polish Art Center
313-874-2242

Jackson
Anna's Unique Gifts
517-783-6010

Lansing
The Mole Hole
517-482-2333

Roseville
World Gardenland
810-771-7700

MINNESOTA
Edina
t.r. christian
800-788-9805

Lindstrom
Gustaf's
800-831-8413

Roseville
Seefeldt's Gallery
651-631-1397

MISSISSIPPI
Columbus
Pitty Pats
888-327-3358

MISSOURI
Kansas City
Hiles Two
800-313-0839

Liberty
Anna Marie's
877-RADKO-KC

Springfield
The Cottage & Provence
888-96-RADKO

St. Charles
Flower Petaler/The Holiday
House
314-946-4027

Weston
Kriss Kringle's
816-333-1530

MONTANA
Bozeman
Montana Gift Corral
800-242-5055

NEW HAMPSHIRE
Amherst
Amherst Shoppe
603-673-1540

Meredith
Christmas Loft
800-962-6180

North Conway
Christmas Loft
800-962-6180

North Woodstock
Christmas Loft
800-962-6180

NEW JERSEY
Eatontown
Weston's Limited Edition
800-509-9424

Haddonfield
Eleanor Vail
609-216-7223

Little Silver
Gift Winds
732-842-5150

Westfield
Williams Nursery
888-88-RADKO

Wyckoff
L'Eglise
201-891-3622

NEW YORK
Clifton Park
Wit's End Giftique
518-371-9273

Fayetteville
Red Geranium
877-277-2831

Huntington
The Gilded Lily
516-673-7955

Merrick
The Limited Edition
800-645-2864

North Tonawanda
Calico Corner
877-694-7575

Pawling
Maple Tree Gallery
877-20-RADKO

NORTH CAROLINA
Calabash
Callahan's Of Calabash
800-344-3816

OHIO
Cincinnati
Story Book Kids
800-228-7636

North Canton
Barthel's Garden Center
330-499-3990
Coach & Four
800-580-4789

Perrysburg
Houck's
419-874-4528

PENNSYLVANIA
Ephrata
Doneckers
800-377-9913

Lahaska
Pine Wreath and Candle
215-794-7060

New Berlin
Gabriel's
800-797-2350

Wilkes-Barre
Dundee Gardens
717-735-5452

SOUTH CAROLINA
Abbeville
Miriam's Southern Accents
864-459-5995

Hilton Head Island
Bailey's
800-476-8856

Lexington
Miller's Ltd.
888-436-4582

Spartanburg
Scarlett's
800-661-4371

TENNESSEE
Chattanooga
Papillon, Inc.
800-249-6153

Gatlinburg
Lindz's
423-436-9426

TEXAS
Austin
Breed & Co.
512-328-3960

Dallas
It's a Wrap
214-520-9727

Fredericksburg
The Christmas Store
800-944-1882

Houston
Haus Edelweiss Inc.
281-440-8458
The TLC Shoppe
800-347-8906

McAllen
Barn White
800-890-7637

Salado
The Christmas Shop
888-947-5561

UTAH
Draper
Wasatch Seasons
800-625-2465

Park City
Quality Interiors & Gifts
800-471-3455

VERMONT
Quechee
Christmas Loft
800-962-6180

Shelburn
Christmas Loft
800-962-6180

VIRGINIA
Alexandria
House in the Country
800-771-8427

Newport News
Anderson's Home and Garden
Showplace
800-801-7844

Norfolk
Christmas Attic
800-771-8460

Williamsburg
Bassett's Classic
Christmas Shop
800-645-1225

WASHINGTON
Olympia
Drees
360-357-7177

Silverdale
Country House & Gardens
360-698-7389

Yakima
Shopkeeper
888-57-RADKO

WEST VIRGINIA
White Sulphur Springs
Christmas at the Depot
The Greenbrier
304-536-1110

WISCONSIN
Mt. Horeb
Olson's Christmas House &
Flower Shop
800-236-3017

Sister Bay
Tannenbaum Holiday Shop
800-804-1495

INDEX OF ORNAMENTS